Rev Margot Thompson
42375 NW Depot St
Banks OR 97106-9056

Children First

Worshipping with the Family of God

Mark Burrows

Children First
Worshipping with the Family of God

ISBN 978-1-426-70775-9

Unless otherwise noted, Scripture quotations are from the New Revised Standard Version of the Bible, copyright 1989, Division of Christian Education of the National Council of the Churches of Christ in the United States of America. Used by permission. All rights reserved.

Scripture quotations marked NIV are taken from the Holy Bible, NEW INTERNATIONAL VERSION®. Copyright © 1973, 1978, 1984 by International Bible Society. All rights reserved throughout the world. Used by permission of International Bible Society.

Lead Editor: Daphna Flegal
Production Editor: Julie P. Glass
Designers: Kellie Green and Keitha Vincent

Art/photo credits—Cover: Michael T. Green; p. 4: J.P. Patin; pp. 5, 91: Photodisc®; p. 6: Hemera Technologies; pp. 7, 9, 13 (both), 16, 86, 93, 94: Jupiterimages®; p. 8: George Doyle; p. 11: Stockbyte®; p. 14: Digital Vision; pp. 15, 17B, 57, 59, 69, 71, 73, 83: Nina Burrows; pp. 17A, 24: Richard Lewisohn; pp. 20, 85: Brand X Pictures®; pp. 22, 89, 96: Comstock® Images; p. 95: BananaStock™

10 11 12 13 14 15 16 17 18 19—10 9 8 7 6 5 4 3 2 1

MANUFACTURED IN THE UNITED STATES OF AMERICA

Contents

What Is *Children First?*

- *Children First* is a worship experience designed specifically for children and their families.

- *Children First* is a 40- to 45-minute service that takes place the first Sunday of every month (Children *First*).

- *Children First* is an opportunity for children to serve in leadership roles.

- *Children First* is a service where children love the energy, the music, the interactive prayers and Bible stories...and so do their parents.

- *Children First* is a service where the parents love the relevant themes, the moments of quiet contemplation, the teaching of some of our church's cherished traditions...and so do their children.

- *Children First* is a worship experience that brings many different styles together successfully. Our children haven't yet learned that classical music is "boring," and we aren't about to tell them.

- *Children First* utilizes art, drama, songs, world drumming, body percussion, storytelling, current events, poetry, and prayer to reinforce a central theme as we help children connect with God.

- *Children First* works hard to create a service that is meaningful and enjoyable for our children. Our hope is that worship will be such a positive experience for them today that worship will always be a major part of their lives.

The Experiment

We wanted to give something a try. Many of us in the church—staff, clergy, and parents—felt that we needed to do more for children in worship. After many years of nudging, we finally had a children's message at the 11:00 A.M. traditional service in the sanctuary. This was a nice first step. Our church is

very traditional, and changes, of any kind, to worship do not come easy. The decision to add the children's message had been put off many times out of anxiety for how some of our members would react. As it turns out, it was a whole lot of worrying over very little. The children responded very well and rushed down to the front of the sanctuary by the dozens (it's not unusual for us to have 70–80 children come to the front) each Sunday. And our adult members have been very supportive.

Photo permission granted by First United Methodist Church, Fort Worth, TX.

Introduction

But as I said, many of us considered this a good "first step." We felt that the children deserved and needed more than just a few minutes devoted to them. Was there a way to make the entire worship service more inviting, more appealing for children? Are children's worship needs any less important than those of the adults?

So one summer Sunday, after months of planning, research, and meetings with focus groups, we held a family service in the sanctuary. Reactions were mixed. There were some who truly enjoyed the service. And there were also those who were very upset and threatened to leave the church if we ever did it again.

One of the most important and difficult things we did was put out a written survey for people to express their opinions. And when you ask for opinions, wow, are you ever going to get them! It was estimated that, of all the people present in worship that morning, 33% turned in completed surveys. That may not seem like a lot, but in the world of surveys, it's huge. Some people were passionate in their opinion that we should not change the traditional worship service that they love. Others were passionate that this kind of service represented a major step for us if we wanted to remain relevant in the twenty-first century. And while the majority had favorable things to say about the service, we certainly had not received a "mandate from the masses" to hold a weekly family-style service.

What the surveys told us was that there was a great deal of interest in a family service, but not every week. We knew that if we had a family service each week, many adults would have to choose between attending worship with their children and attending a Sunday school class where they may have been members for many years. We felt it very important for parents to attend worship with their children as often as possible, so we wanted to take this difficult choice out of the equation.

We decided to offer a family service once each month—the first Sunday, so it would be easy to remember. The service would take place in our chapel, a space available from 9:30–10:30 A.M., that would keep us from disrupting any already-existent traditional services in the sanctuary. We then went to the adult Sunday schools where the majority of the children's parents attended and asked if they would be willing to forego Sunday school once a month to participate in worship with their children. They all agreed!

What started as an experiment has now become one of our church's biggest success stories. When we started to hold *Children First* services, the chapel would be half full. Now we routinely pack the space, and have even had several "standing room only" services. We are currently looking for a larger space to accommodate our family service and the community it has helped to foster. This is a very good second step. But in my opinion, our work isn't done. I still believe that family worship should occur on a weekly basis. And it is my hope that the energy, enthusiasm, and goodwill generated by our monthly *Children First* services will inspire our church to take that next great step together…as a true family.

The Elements of Worship

The following pages describe the elements of worship that we use in the *Children First* worship services, along with an explanation of how we use each one.

Gathering and Prelude

Our *Children First* services start at 9:45 A.M. in our chapel. Every week there is an early service in the chapel that doesn't finish until 9:30 A.M. That leaves us a whopping fifteen minutes to "reset the space" for an entirely different style of worship, while making sure that all the children and families who come through our doors feel welcomed and appreciated. This is no small feat, and it takes a true team effort to do it all well.

There are two entrances into the chapel. At each entrance an usher hands out bulletins, and a greeter welcomes everyone who walks through the door. All four of these volunteers are children.

Meanwhile, other members of the worship team are busy preparing the space by setting up banners, altar pieces, the puppet stage, music stands, microphones, and anything else that needs to be in place. Somehow or another, this all gets done by about 9:40 A.M. At this point the keyboardist starts playing prelude music as more and more children and their families arrive. We have one of those great keyboardists who knows, almost intuitively, when to start playing. And with a simple nod of the head from one of the worship leaders, she can bring whatever piece she is playing to a close as if it were written that way.

Announcements

Announcements in *Children First* are always very brief. If there is an upcoming family event, such as a children's choir concert or a fall festival, we highlight it. Otherwise, we skip the announcement segment entirely.

Remember that every minute you spend at the beginning of the service is a minute you pay for at the end of the service. The congregation may sit attentively for several announcements at the beginning, because it's at the beginning. But by the time the benediction comes around, you'll have a lot more children wiggling and parents looking at watches (and in some cases, parents wiggling too).

Keep announcements short.

Group Singing

This segment of the *Children First* service is when things really get cooking! Group Singing almost always consists of three songs, all related to the theme in an intentional way. (The recorded music, sheet music, and PowerPoint® presentations of the music lyrics are available on the CD-ROM included with this resource.)

The first two songs are up-tempo, and usually in a more modern style. Because these songs are more modern, they tend to be less familiar to the congregation. That means the song leaders must do a little teaching so that everyone can feel comfortable enough to participate.

Learning one song during a worship service can be fun and invigorating for worship participants. But learning two songs in a row can feel tedious and derail the forward momentum you're trying to establish. When we know we're going to introduce one song that is brand-new to everyone, we make sure the other song is at least somewhat familiar. A campfire song or a piggyback (parody) song that uses a familiar melody with the new words printed in the bulletin is a good complement to a brand-new song.

Another type of song that works well in this spot is a call-and-response song. In this type of song, the leader sings a line and the congregation sings a simple response. The leader then sings a different line, but the congregation always sings the same response. It doesn't take long to teach the response. And before you know it, you're all singing a song together. A similar type of song, an echo song, is even easier to get going. The song leader simply asks the congregation to echo whatever he or she sings.

At least one of the first two songs (if not both) must incorporate simple movement. Children need to move. People need to move. This doesn't have to be anything fancy. Simply clapping or stomping to the beat is movement, so is physically depicting the words to a song like "Deep and Wide." And there are times when bringing in some American Sign Language can add a wonderful new dimension to a song.

The third song in the Group-Singing segment is always the processional hymn. This is two or three verses of a more traditional hymn, usually from the hymnal.

Conventional wisdom might hold that children who are used to singing and moving to up-tempo, modern songs will tune out these older (read "boring") hymns. But that hasn't been my observation. If anything, the energy amassed from the first two songs carries over into the processional hymn so that all are singing "lustily and with good courage."

The song leaders often invite the parents and other adults to sing out strong on these more traditional hymns. In a sense, the adults are being asked to help teach our children some of the great traditional songs of our faith.

The adults seem to truly embrace this role as they help pass on this great music to our next generation. And the children get a kick out of hearing the grownups really sing out. And since the children are gaining exposure to these traditional hymns in a more invitational way, they are less likely to be intimidated when they hear these same hymns in the great big sanctuary.

Something that adds a great deal to the processional hymn is the presence of acolytes. These children symbolically bring the light of the world into our midst as they process down the aisle and light the altar candles. This is no small thing, by the way. How many of us remember as acolytes being terrified that our taper would go out before we even got down to the altar? Or worse yet, we'd get all the way down, and with the whole congregation watching, the candles wouldn't light!

I love watching the acolytes come down the aisle. Even the bounciest kiddos among us treat the role of acolyte with wonder and respect. It's a beautiful thing.

Opening Prayer

The Opening Prayer is spoken by the entire congregation, and relates directly to the theme. We utilize many different types of prayers in *Children First,* including unison prayers, call-and-response prayers, body prayers, breath prayers, sung prayers, poem prayers, blues prayers, sign-language prayers, litanies, and more (see pages 84–95). There are so many ways to pray beyond the "Okay, children; let's all close our eyes, bow our heads, and fold our hands" prayers.

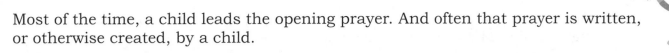

Most of the time, a child leads the opening prayer. And often that prayer is written, or otherwise created, by a child.

Theme for the Day

One of the most exciting parts of the service is when the Theme for the Day is revealed. If the worship participants have been paying close attention during the Group Singing and the Opening Prayer, they're likely to already have a pretty good idea what the theme is.

Prior to the service, we invite a child artist to create a sign on posterboard or foam board with the theme written on one side in very large letters. The child may also decorate the sign with pictures or symbols appropriate to the theme. And the lettering can be any color, as long as it is legible from the back of the worship space.

A different child is responsible for revealing the Theme for the Day during *Children First.* (We don't print the theme in the bulletin. We like for the worship participants to guess what the theme is based on the Group Singing and Opening Prayer. Then when the theme is revealed, people get to see how close their guesses were. This is just one more small way to engage our worship participants.) She or he will come to the front, holding the poster face-down.

All the worship participants use their laps as drums and create a big, loud drumroll. Then they stop, and the child holds up the poster revealing the theme as he or she shouts the theme very loudly. It's such a dramatic (and fun) element that we always do it twice in a row. This is a great role for a younger child volunteer.

By the way, about the theme—we try to make the theme one word whenever possible, two words at most.

For those of us planning out the service, this really helps us to focus on the core of the message. For example, one recent December the worship team started out with the theme, Christmas Around the World. The scriptural springboard for us was the account of the wise men found in Matthew 2.

Planning went as you might expect—Christmas carols from this country and that, exploration of different customs. We were planning something fun, festive, and colorful, but what was our core message? What did we want worship participants to walk away thinking about? We needed to narrow our focus a bit.

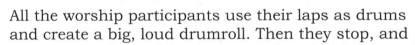

One of the best ways to narrow our focus is by using that time-tested method of the two-year-old—"why logic." We kept asking "why" until we got to the heart of it all.

"Why are we here?"   "To celebrate Christmas around the world."

"Why?"   "To help us remember the journey of the wise men."

"Why?"   "Because they came from distant lands."

"Why?"   "To worship Jesus."

"Why?"   "Because Jesus was a special person, born for all the world."

"Why?"   "Because God loves all of us."

Like with any two-year-old, you can get stuck going in circles with this. The trick is to find the point where you've asked enough "whys" that the service has real focus, yet there's still enough room to ask a few more "whys" during the service itself. If you notice, in our "why logic" exercise, the word "all" started popping up. Aha!

So we revealed *All* as the theme for that particular service. Then we spent the rest of the service explaining what we meant by that. And from the standpoint of the worship participants, this created an exciting sense of mystery.

Also, narrowing the focus helped us keep from getting lost in the details. For example, how many of us have "taught" the story of Jonah by reading the story in five minutes, then spending the next 45 minutes on some great fish-related craft? Is that what the story of Jonah is really all about? With a Christmas-Around-the-World theme, we could have easily gotten lost among all the crowns, camels, and frankincense.

Rest assured, the wise men still made an appearance in our *All* service, as did Christmas carols from England, Germany, Liberia, the United States, and Spain. But each of these elements, rather than being ends unto themselves, contributed to a greater end in teaching and reinforcing the very important message that the birth of Jesus was for all.

Sign of the Day

Not to be confused with the Theme for the Day, the Sign of the Day refers to American Sign Language. Immediately after the theme is revealed, another child comes forward and teaches all in attendance how to sign the theme.

(This is yet another reason why a one-word theme is so helpful.)

The child demonstrates the sign, and the worship participants get to practice signing the theme, often multiple times.

For example, one November the theme was *Thank You*. A child came forward and taught us the sign for "thank you."

Then the worship participants were asked to say "thank you" in sign language to many people there.

Let's sign "thank you" to our Sunday school teachers who teach us so much.

Now let's sign "thank you" to Sara who plays the piano so beautifully for us each service.

We must have signed "thank you" to ten people or groups of people.

Children respond so wonderfully to sign language. It's beautiful, it's expressive, and it's physical.

There are also many instances where the worship participants are asked to remember the sign for later on in the service. For instance, during a service on *Love,*

the worship participants had been taught the sign for "love." Much later in the service, there was a Scripture reading where the word "love" appeared numerous times. Before reading the Scripture, the worship participants were invited to sign the word "love" every time they heard it read.

This had two major benefits. First of all, it reinforced the sign they had been taught earlier in the service, making retention more likely. Secondly, the Scripture by itself can often "lose" the very young among us. By inviting everyone to sign the word "love" whenever they heard it read, we created an environment much more conducive to active listening. Even the littlest ears tend to tune in whenever we do something like that.

Two online resources we use often are *www.aslpro.com* and *www.handspeak.com*. These show how to sign most of the words or phrases we use in *Children First*. By far the best resource is a person in your community who can either sign for your worship services or teach children how to sign the themes.

Good News

Good News is one of the most important, uplifting, and popular elements of our *Children First* services. Yet it wasn't even a part of the original *Children First* concept until one night when I happened upon a scene that shook me to the core.

I was driving home late one night after choir rehearsal. While driving through a residential area not far from my home, I saw two people crouched over what appeared to be a lump in the middle of the street. My immediate thought was, "Oh, those poor people. Their cat or dog must've wandered into the street and been hit by a car."

As I slowly drove by, I looked over and noticed that it wasn't a pet, it was a person. So I pulled over and got out to see how I could help; 9-1-1 had already been called and help was on the way. The person lying on the ground was an elderly woman whose son, in a drug-induced stupor, chased her out of the house, beating her with a rock. One of the people crouched over her, confused and weeping, was her husband. The other was a neighbor who had heard the disturbance and was now holding the woman's hand. The son had run away and was still on the loose.

Eventually, paramedics arrived and took the woman to the nearest hospital. I later learned that she died on the way.

By the time I got home, it was very late. My wife was still awake and worried. I recounted the series of events, trembling the entire time. This had all happened literally blocks from our house. I was not feeling particularly confident about humanity's inherent goodness. How could someone do this to another person—to his own mother? What is the matter with people?!

It's amazing what sleep can do for the brain, for the soul. The next morning I woke up and started playing through the events again in my head. Something awful had happened. A life had been taken, and other lives had been changed forever by one terrible act. But then I started to remember other things, other people. I remembered the neighbor who was crouched over the elderly woman, holding her hand through it all. I remembered another neighbor running out of her house with a blanket to keep the woman warm. I remember several more neighbors pouring out of their houses to ask what had happened and what they could do. Many offered to give the woman's husband a ride to the hospital and stay with him. Some worked with police, giving descriptions of the son who was still out there. Some prayed. All seemed genuinely concerned.

For all the bad in the world, there is so much more that is good. For one who would seek to hurt, there are so many more that would do anything to help. It can be difficult at times to remember that. The nightly news doesn't exactly help. The occasional water-skiing squirrel aside, we're painted a

pretty grim picture of society, aren't we? The sensational act of violence or the words of hate may make the lead story, but they do not tell the whole story. There is so much good news out there that children need to know about, that we all need to know about. So we decided to add a segment to our fledgling worship service that focused on the good news.

When we started out, each Good-News segment consisted of three short stories, one about something good happening in our world, one about something good happening in our community (city, area), and one about something good happening in our church.

A week prior to the service, three children were asked to serve as Good-News "reporters" in charge of gathering the stories. The Good-News stories had to be about something current, and they had to relate to the worship theme.

An adult, serving as the Good-News "editor," would meet with the reporters before the service to go over their stories. The child reporters delivered the Good News during the worship service, and the editor served as a sort of anchor, helping the segment flow and making the reporters feel more at ease in front of the rest of the worship participants.

Sometimes the adult editor would ask the worship participants to reach under their seats and pull out their invisible "Good-News goggles," and put them on as they listened to the Good News. Once it was "Good-News socks." It was a nice touch.

Over the course of time, however, we observed that we were losing the attention of some of our worship participants. Unless we had the equivalent of child actors up there delivering the Good News, it felt a little like school book reports. The stories were great, and the children were certainly earnest in their delivery. But it just wasn't resonating like we'd hoped. In our post-worship evaluation meetings, we all agreed that the Good-News segment was where we were seeing the biggest dip in energy. We needed to adjust.

It was early April, and we were planning our May service where the theme was *Prayer*. Doing Good-News stories about prayer in our world, our community, and our church didn't seem to fit for some reason. So we decided to try something different.

We invited three children to speak about a time when they prayed—what they prayed for and why. The adult "editor" would serve more as an interviewer, asking each child the question, following up or clarifying if necessary, but mostly hanging back and letting the children take the lead. The stories the children told about prayer were personal, powerful, and deeply heartfelt. They weren't just telling a story; they were a vital part of the story. And those who had been losing interest in the segment the previous month were all sitting forward in their seats with rapt attention. Aha!

Most of the time, this is how we structure the Good News—in an interview format. It works beautifully. What had once been one of the low-energy points of the *Children First* service has now become a major highlight. It is one of the few segments that regularly gets applause. Not that applause is necessarily the best indicator of the success of a worship element. But there's no denying the worship participants are really paying attention.

Another addition we made to the Good-News segment is a sort of intro/outro to the segment based on a simple call-and-response a few of us learned while working with a children's choir in Kenya. Here's how it goes.

Leader: God is good,
Group: All the time.
Leader: All the time,
Group: God is good.

In the village of Kianjai where we visited, after the group responded, "God is good," they continued: "And that's God's nature. Wow!" We were so grateful to the children for teaching us the call-and-response. We taught them how to make the word WOW with their faces. By holding up three fingers in each hand, you make the Ws. You then hold these hands on either side of your face, while opening your mouth for the O. WOW! They loved it—a successful cultural exchange!

The children who attend the *Children First* service insist on doing the part where they get to say, "Wow!" It's easy, memorable, physical...and fun!

This call-and-response also serves as a great transition activity. While the worship participants are doing the call-and-response, the Good-News reporters and editor are gathering at the front. Likewise, we do the call-and-response at the end of the Good-News segment as the reporters and editor go back to their seats, and the volunteers for the next segment get in place.

Expression of Faith

The original concept for the Expression-of-Faith segment was a different form of artistic expression for each service. One month it could be a piano solo. The next month it could be a

children's choir or a dance or any other form of artistic expression, as long as it somehow reflects the Theme for the Day.

Most of the time, however, the Expression-of-Faith segment is the home of our multi-age puppetry troupe, Threadbare Theatre.

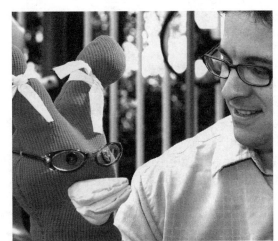

All of the puppets used in Threadbare Theatre are constructed from household objects and recycled materials, thus the term "threadbare." The Verdi Family, a group of five wooden-spoon puppets, performs comic mini-operas on anger management and loving our neighbors. Shadow puppets, projected onto the walls using overhead projectors, portray Bible stories. But by far the most popular puppets, especially with our younger children, are Wendell and Lorraine. These are two recurring characters portrayed by more traditional, though still handmade, hand puppets.

The two characters were created to complement each other. Wendell is very sweet and gentle. His capacity for empathy makes him intensely compassionate, but also very sensitive. Lorraine is also good-natured, but lives a little more "in her head" than Wendell. While she is book-smart, she isn't always tuned in to the feelings of others.

These personality differences are just enough to create some mild conflicts which are resolved (or at least addressed) during their scenes. Wendell and Lorraine are each written to approximately represent a kindergarten-aged child.

These two act out "A Day in the Life of a Child" scenes set in a school, a park, or at home. The scenes cover topics relevant to the lives of children, such as coping with change, making new friends, learning to say "I'm sorry," celebrating birthdays, and dealing with friends moving away. The scene, as with every other element of *Children First,* reflects the Theme for the Day.

Here are a few guidelines we follow when developing the puppets scripts:

1. Incorporate as much action as possible. Puppetry is a physical art form. If the scripts are too "talk-talk," then the children will eventually lose interest.

2. Keep the scripts short. This is for two reasons. First of all, we would rather have people want more rather than less. Secondly, we have a tight creative cycle. We usually get together the Sunday afternoon after a *Children First* service to develop the script for the following month. We outline the script based around the theme for the next service. By the following Sunday, we have a rough draft. The puppeteers have a week to go through the script. The

following Sunday is for read-through and blocking. The last week is for running the scene from memory. The more we write, the more we have to memorize.

3. Don't write anything preachy for the puppets. We prefer to have our puppet characters "live out" their faith. It's the responsibility of the adult worship leaders to make the necessary connections between what the puppets act out and how God's Word is relevant to our lives as followers of Christ.

In this resource we've included numerous puppet scripts, including several Wendell-and-Lorraine scenes, and even a few spoon-puppet operas, complete with sheet music (see pages 56–82).

We do occasionally find that puppetry doesn't mesh well with a particular theme. In these cases, other art forms have worked very well in the Expression-of-Faith segment. Here are a few examples.

For our service on *Prayer*, we invited an artist to set up at the front of the worship space and work on a painted prayer during the entire service. She had done little prep work prior to the service, mainly painting some of the background, so that she could complete the painting by the end of the service.

During the Expression-of-Faith time, the artist came forward and answered some questions about what she was painting and why. She had chosen as her subject a bird's nest. For her, the nest is like nature's bowl and a means of receiving grace. Her work provided a gentle visual throughout the entire service. It wasn't wham-bang, fast-paced imagery; yet everyone from the older adults to the youngest children was completely engaged.

For our service on *Remember*, we had Communion. We had a baker, our very own director of children's ministries, behind a table at the front of the worship space, kneading dough for bread. True to cooking-show form, she brought a few loaves that she had baked earlier. These loaves were used as the bread for Communion (as well as a gluten-free option from the grocery store).

The dough she spent the entire service kneading was baked into loaves right after the service at 10:30 A.M. (The sweet smell filled the children's area.) Each child got to have a slice of fresh, hot, buttered bread before leaving at noon.

For our service on *Different,* we had a recorder consort play during the Expression-of-Faith segment. The Scripture for the service was the familiar text about the body of Christ from 1 Corinthians 12 ("If the whole body were an eye, where would the hearing be?..." [12:17]).

The consort started with everyone in the group playing the melody. The tune was recognizable, but the overall sound wasn't very interesting. Then the whole consort played the bass line—pretty boring. Then they all played the tenor line—still boring. Then the members of the recorder consort each played their own parts. When everyone contributed their own, different line to the whole, the result was a beautiful, rich sound.

Puppet Scripts

There are several puppet scripts (see pages 56–71). Most of the scripts are written for two characters. A puppetry group within our church, Threadbare Theatre, performs the majority of the characters.

Many scripts feature the two recurring characters, Wendell and Lorraine. When we know in advance that the puppeteer for either Wendell or Lorraine will not be available for a particular service, we either introduce a new character or write a script for puppet and human.

We use puppets we've constructed out of recycled and other household materials. But you can use just about anything, including store-bought puppets. When Abingdon Press releases their VBS curriculum each year, there is a corresponding hand puppet. If you keep all of those VBS characters, over the course of a few summers, you should have a nice assortment of puppets you can use.

Also included are scripts for two Spoon-Puppet Operas, complete with the music (see pages 72–82 and CD-ROM). The actions for these mini-operas are performed by one adult and one child puppeteer with wooden spoons.

A narrator moves the action along, while one of the song leaders sings all the arias. Some of the words in the narration are in bold text. These are appropriate places for action within the show. We use five wooden spoons with painted faces. But the truth is, you don't really need faces on the spoons...or even spoons, for that matter. You can use spoons, spatulas, Ping-Pong paddles...just about anything with a handle on it (well, maybe not chain saws!).

Incidentally, we don't use a puppet stage, mainly because we don't need it. A puppet stage can take up a lot of space, and takes more time to set up than we typically have. We perform everything "cabaret style," where the puppeteers are completely visible. No one minds this, especially not the children. The human imagination is an amazing thing, and within a few seconds, most of the worship participants have forgotten that we humans are even there.

We Believe

This is the time when we as a faith community, led by a child, stand and profess what we believe. In our particular setting, the one that seems to work best is "A Statement of Faith of the United Church of Canada." Use what works best in your setting.

We are not alone, we live in God's world.
We believe in God:
> who has created and is creating,
> who has come in Jesus, the Word made flesh,
> to reconcile and make new,
> who works in us and others by the Spirit.
We trust in God.
We are called to be the Church:
> to celebrate God's presence,
> to live with respect in Creation,
> to love and serve others,
> to seek justice and resist evil,
> to proclaim Jesus, crucified and risen,
> our judge and our hope.
In life, in death, in life beyond death,
> God is with us. We are not alone.
Thanks be to God. Amen.

["A New Creed," The United Church of Canada. Cited March 25, 2010, *http://www.united-church.ca/beliefs/creed.* Used with permission.]

This affirmation is commonly utilized in our traditional services. So when our children participate in worship in the sanctuary, this is an element that will seem somewhat familiar.

As accessible as this affirmation is, it is still a lot of text. To help, I usually invite the worship participants to pay special attention to one keyword or

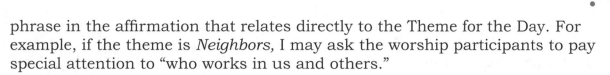

phrase in the affirmation that relates directly to the Theme for the Day. For example, if the theme is *Neighbors,* I may ask the worship participants to pay special attention to "who works in us and others."

We are currently working on a project with several children to create their own statements of faith.

Gloria Patri

The singing of the Gloria Patri is another element which is part of our traditional services. Our more tradition-minded members really appreciate this. And for those who prefer more modern musical forms, we remind them that the Gloria Patri is truly one of the world's greatest and most enduring praise choruses.

The Gloria Patri serves as a wonderful follow-up to the affirmation of faith because it gives us the chance to sing praise to those in whom we place our faith and trust.

> Glory be to the Father
> and to the Son
> and to the Holy Ghost;
> as it was in the beginning,
> is now, and ever shall be,
> world without end.
> Amen. Amen.
>
> [Words: Lesser Doxology, 3rd-4th cent.]

Musical Call to Prayer

The Call to Prayer is a musical transition into a quieter, more contemplative portion of the worship service. This short piece is sung by a soloist or duet, and is always soft and gentle. And the text, of course, reflects the Theme for the Day.

We don't expect everyone to go from super-active to contemplative at the snap of our fingers. This element, often combined with the slight dimming of the lights, helps set an atmosphere of calm and stillness. A few musical selections for the Call to Prayer are provided in this resource (see CD-ROM).

Time for Reflection

It is vital to plan time for quiet contemplation in our services. We can get so stuck trying to "amp it up" in order to keep the children engaged, that we might forget the children also need, even crave, moments of stillness. And that doesn't mean that any energy has been lost; it's just been channeled inward.

Once the last notes of the Call to Prayer have faded, I always invite the worship participants to take in a deep, cleansing breath through the nose and quietly sigh it out. We do this two or three times. This kind of intentional breathing, as opposed to merely inhaling and exhaling, does as much to bring calm to the room as providing soothing music or dimming the lights.

After a few seconds of silence (and yes, even with a room full of children, it can get pretty quiet), we focus on something related to our theme. For the service on *Love,* I asked everyone to think of someone whom they love. Then I invited each of them to use a finger to trace the name (or make an imaginary picture) of that person in the palm of their other hand. Next, I invited them to take their palm and gently place it on their heart and whisper, "love." Finally, I invited them to sit for a few moments and think about that person, and how they could show their love to that person.

The pacing of the Time for Reflection is deliberate, and I try not to speak much louder than a whisper. It's as much about tone as it is about content.

For our service on *Anger Management,* we passed out Crayola® Model Magic® to each of the worship participants. I challenged them to think about something or someone that made them angry. Next, I invited each of them to knead their Crayola® Model Magic®, and as they did so, to release some of the anger they felt for that circumstance or person. It was quiet and contemplative, yet it was still engaging and quite physical. After a few more moments of silence, I lead the Lord's Prayer as the worship participants join in.

The Lord's Prayer

We have spent the last few minutes exploring our individual joys and concerns. Reciting the Lord's Prayer in unison is a powerful way to bring the group back together. When we hear all those voices around us reciting the same prayer, it reminds us that we don't face all of our challenges alone.

We are never too young to start learning this important lesson. The Lord's Prayer is packed with so much, and we have our whole lives to explore its meaning and importance.

Musical Prayer Response

Like the Call to Prayer, the Prayer Response is sung by a soloist or duet. In fact, most of the time, the Prayer Response is the second verse of the music used for the Call to Prayer, creating a sort of "bookend" for this more contemplative section of the *Children First* service.

Scripture/Bible Story

What does the Bible have to say about it? This is a question we ask during the planning phase of every *Children First* service. As we explore everyday issues, from promises to peer pressure to anger management, it is vital for our worship participants to understand the role that Scripture plays in our lives.

The Bible isn't just an old, beautiful book with old, beautiful words. The Bible is here to help us, to guide us, to comfort us, to energize us, to challenge us, to teach us…today! We passionately believe this.

The problem was that we were conveying this passionate belief through pretty dispassionate means—the dry reading of Scripture. You can imagine how this went over with the worship participants, especially the younger ones. Compared with singing songs, signing the theme, watching puppets, and participating in experiential prayers, sitting to listen as someone read from the Bible could seem (dare I say it) boring. That's not to say that reading Scripture, in and of itself, is necessarily boring. An excellent reader can do much to bring the story to life.

But we still couldn't help noticing a palpable dip in the energy level of the service. We were unintentionally sending the message that while the rest of the time is fun, colorful, and interactive, Bible time is sit-down, don't-wiggle, be-quiet time. We wanted our children to turn to Scripture, not tune it out.

We spent time looking for ways to make the rewording of Scripture more engaging. We wanted to transform this element of the service from have-to to highlight.

Here are some of the ways we have found to bring the story to life:

Shadow Puppets—Recruit a few children to use black card stock to cut out simple figures for use in a shadow-puppet portrayal of a Bible story. An overhead projector can cast the shadows onto a screen or blank wall. We used shadow puppets to tell the story of the visit of the wise men.

Pantomime—Recruit a few children to silently pantomime the actions of a Bible story. Be careful with this. Make sure the actions in the story are appropriate for young people to perform. A variation on this would be to have the children create a few freeze-frame scenes (tableaux) from the Bible story.

Storyboards—Recruit a few children to each select a portion of a Bible story, such as the parable of the good Samaritan, and illustrate that portion of the story on separate pieces of posterboard.

Then, during the reading of the Bible story, have each child stand at the front of the worship space and reveal his or her picture at the appropriate time. It only takes three or four pictures to illustrate most Bible stories. Plus, it is one more way to involve children in the design and leadership of the worship service.

Expressive Play—During a service about differences, we read the 1 Corinthians 12 Scripture about the body of Christ ("If the whole body were an eye, where would the hearing be?..." [12:17]). One person read the Scripture while another sculpted a Mr. Potato Head®, first with nothing but feet, then with nothing but eyes, before finally making a Mr. Potato Head® with all the parts of the body.

Listening/Signing—This is a good way to not only make a Scripture reading more engaging, but also to reinforce the Sign for the Day from earlier in the service. For example, the Scripture 1 Corinthians 13:1-8 contains the word "love" seven times. Before reading the Scripture, remind the worship participants how to sign "love." Then invite them to make the sign every time they hear it read.

Bible Memory Verse

This is usually, though not always, taken from the Scripture or Bible story. It is never more than one or two sentences.

We set the Bible memory verse to a simple, catchy rhythm. A leader teaches the worship participants how to speak the verse in rhythm while they pat the rhythm on their laps. We call it playing their "lap drums."

The trick is to repeat the verse in rhythm many times, without allowing it to feel repetitious. We will repeat the verse in rhythm as many as twelve times, doing it a different way each time. Here are a few options.

Speak the verse while patting.
Speak the verse while clapping.
Speak the verse while stomping.
Speak the verse while snapping fingers. (Younger children may find this difficult.)

Speak the verse loudly.
Speak the verse softly.
Speak the verse in a high voice.
Speak the verse in a low voice.
Speak the verse in a silly voice.
Speak the verse quickly.
Speak the verse in super slow motion.
Speak the verse with mouths closed.
Blink the rhythm of the verse.
Tongue-click the rhythm of the verse.
Clap the rhythm of the verse.
Tap noses to the rhythms of the verse.

In those last few, the worship participants aren't speaking the words of the verse in an audible way, but they are thinking the words. This is an important step for internalizing the memory verse. Plus, it's fun, engaging, and gives everyone a chance to participate in a physically active way.

Teaching Moment

The preacher picks a sermon topic. Then, based on that topic, all the other elements from the hymns to the prayers are selected. The sermon is the focal point of the service. Right? That's certainly how it seems to be in most of the churches where I've worked or visited. It's all about the sermon. Everything else radiates from there.

For awhile, we even tried to squeeze *Children First* into this model. You know what we discovered? It doesn't really fit. We adults on the worship-planning team had been conditioned for years to believe that every worship service needed a sermon. Why should *Children First* be any different? Sure, we would make it a children's sermon, and we would call it "Teaching Moment" rather than a sermon. But it would still be the time, about two-thirds through the service, when someone would get up to do some extended talking. How do you think it turned out?

Even when we planned a fun, active Teaching Moment, it still seemed to fall short. So we started asking, "Do we really need the Teaching Moment?" When we stayed true to the theme through every other element of the service, we found the Teaching Moment wasn't really necessary.

This notion was confirmed one Sunday when we were running behind on time. We decided to cut the Teaching Moment altogether. We didn't mention it or make a big deal of it. We simply skipped ahead to the next element in the service. Now, we all know good and well that in church, when we cut something that someone really likes, we're going to hear about it. Guess what? Nobody said a thing about it. What a telling silence that was.

We still have a Teaching Moment on occasion. Sometimes we find a children's sermon that's too perfect for the theme to pass up. Sometimes we need an "Act II" time slot for a Wendell-and-Lorraine story line. But one thing we do not do is keep the Teaching Moment in the service just because the service "has to" have one.

For help with Teaching Moments that correspond with the *Children First* themes, check out *Wow Time: 52 Engaging Children's Moments,* by Mark Burrows (ISBN: 9781426707926).

Offertory

We do take up an offering at every *Children First* service. Children always serve as ushers, and they take their role very seriously. In fact, every month I get calls from parents whose children want to serve as ushers.

During the offering we always have some music for the Offertory. In the past it has been, among other things, a vocal solo by a child or adult, an instrumental solo by a child, a children's choir, or a children's percussion ensemble.

One of the most powerful musical offerings was for our *Forever* service that coincided with All Saints' Day. The children's choir prepared a special piece to sing. And in the weeks leading up to the service, they brought photos of friends, family, and pets that lived far away or had moved away or died. One parent created a slide show with the photos that was played while the children's choir sang.

Another memorable Offertory was an intergenerational piece sung by the children's choir and their mothers and special friends.

We periodically send out surveys to find what talents, musical and otherwise, our worship participants may possess. It's always amazing to learn what people can do. And quite often, with a little encouragement, they are willing to share those talents to the benefit of worship and the glory of God.

Doxology

This is another of the great hymns of praise that is a part of our church's traditional services. It gives the worship participants a chance to stand and sing—something they haven't done for about ten minutes of worship time.

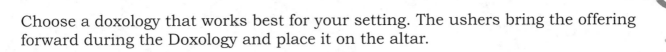

Choose a doxology that works best for your setting. The ushers bring the offering forward during the Doxology and place it on the altar.

Prayer over the Gifts

Immediately after the Doxology, a child leads us in a prayer over the offering. Sometimes it is an original prayer spoken by the child alone. Often it is the following prayer which the congregation joins in reciting.

> All of our treasures
> We joyfully give—
> The prayers that we whisper,
> The lives that we live.
>
> Our time and our talents,
> Our hands and our hearts—
> God, you gave these to us,
> Now we'll do our part.
> Amen.

Closing Songs

This is group singing that usually consists of two songs. The first is one of the songs from the Group Singing at the beginning of the service. We normally select the most active of the Group-Singing songs. By this point in the service, the children (and adults) really need to move. And the singing here is always robust because now it's a song with which the worship participants are familiar.

The second song serves as a sort of "song of farewell." Two appropriate choices here are "Let There Be Peace on Earth" and "Shalom."

Benediction

This is led by a child. We almost always use the same benediction, which is a tradition in our church.

> Leader: Our gathering will soon be ended.
>   Where will we go, and what will we do?
> **People: We will go out to be God's people in the world.**
> Leader: May grace, peace, hope, love, and joy
>   forever accompany us. Amen.

Postlude

Everyone sits for the Postlude, which is usually a short, up-tempo piece played by our talented keyboardist. Sitting for the Postlude is not something they do in the traditional services in the sanctuary, much to the chagrin of the organist.

We are trying to teach the children that the Postlude isn't "exit music." It's yet one more way to stay connected to the worship experience. Sure, there's some wiggling. There are also many, including children, who appreciate the extra minute of reflection.

Getting Ready

Each *Children First* service requires a great deal of preparation. And that preparation takes place in stages.

Six to Twelve Months Out—We carefully select the themes for each service. One of the first things we do is take a look at the calendar and determine if any special days fall on the first Sunday of the month. For example, All Saints' Sunday is typically the first Sunday in November. So one November, our *Children First* service, *Forever,* took that into account. One year Palm Sunday fell on the first Sunday of April, so our theme was *Celebrate.*

Then we consider other times of the year and their significance in the lives of our worship participants, especially our children. The first Sunday in September, *Learn* was our theme, to coincide with back-to-school.

Once we've taken these special times of year into consideration, we determine what other worship themes will resonate with our families. This is more than merely a few people in an office coming up with themes. It's a multistep process that involves many people. We start with a list of over eighty potential themes. Then a small but varied group narrows that list down to about twenty potential themes. Then a much larger group narrows that list down even more until we get to twelve themes—one each month for a year. Each step in this process involves parents, clergy, our director of children's ministries, and yes, children. It's interesting to note how adults will try to choose themes they think the children will like. These are often very different from what the children themselves choose. *Quiet Time* was a theme that got very few adult votes. But it got so many votes from the children that it made the top twelve.

And when I'm polling children, I like to do so over the phone, with their parents' permission. I've found, as you can imagine, that when I ask a child's opinion in front of others, many of them say what they think others want them to say—what they think is expected of them.

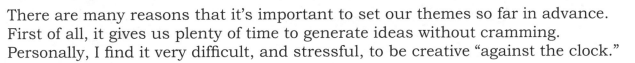

There are many reasons that it's important to set our themes so far in advance. First of all, it gives us plenty of time to generate ideas without cramming. Personally, I find it very difficult, and stressful, to be creative "against the clock."

Secondly, once we have good ideas, we can identify people with the talents to make those ideas come to life. And we have time to gather any materials we need.

Lastly, we coordinate worship and education. Whatever our theme is for a *Children First* service will be the theme for children's Sunday school the rest of the month. Knowing the themes well in advance gives our teachers a chance to plan or acquire appropriate curriculum.

Three to Six Months Out—We determine which services will involve music from one of our children's choirs. It takes weeks to properly prepare a choir to sing a piece in worship. Careful planning with our children's choir director helps her plan her rehearsal schedule effectively, which sets the children up for success, and we all benefit as a result. And since we already know the themes well in advance, the choir director can select pieces that best reflect those themes.

One Month Out—We select all the specific elements for the service, such as songs, hymns, prayers, and litanies. We generate a short puppet script, if needed, for the Expression of Faith.

We also secure all our adult helpers. Many of our most-talented volunteers have to do quite a bit of work-related travel. By one month out, most know their travel plans, but surprises do happen. "One Month Out" means we have very recently had a *Children First* service. Usually, the afternoon immediately after the service, we devote a good amount of time to evaluation of that service.

Three Weeks Out—We give the sheet music to our musicians, hold rehearsals for Expression of Faith as needed, and recruit children to help lead in the following worship areas:

❑ Lead the Opening Prayer
❑ Reveal the Theme for the Day
❑ Create the poster with the Theme for the Day
❑ Demonstrate the Sign for the Day
❑ Good-News Reporters (three children)
❑ Lead the Affirmation of Faith
❑ Be part of the Scripture/Bible-Story Reading by creating and showing storyboards, acting out a Bible story, and so forth.
❑ Lead the Prayer over the Gifts
❑ Lead the Benediction
❑ Serve as acolytes
❑ Serve as greeters
❑ Serve as ushers

Make sure to get parents' permission. I can go into any children's classroom and get a dozen children willing to volunteer. But someone has to drive them to the church and make sure they aren't out of town that weekend.

Two Weeks Out—Get all bulletin information, including names of all worship leaders and helpers, ready for printing. Get theme to children's ministry area. Each month, one children's Sunday school class gets the theme in advance. Each child in the class makes a picture based on the theme. We select the picture that we feel (this is highly subjective) best captures the essence of the theme. Notice I did not say that we pick the prettiest picture.

One Week Out—We call to remind all worship leaders and helpers. This means adults as well as children. We rehearse for Expression of Faith as needed.

8:00 A.M., The Morning Of—We meet with the children who have volunteered to design the Theme-for-the-Day poster and any Scripture/Bible-Story support, such as storyboards or shadow puppets.

8:30 A.M., The Morning Of—All worship leaders and adult helpers report to our rehearsal room at 8:30 A.M. for the 9:45 A.M. service.

We go through all the songs together. Since most of the child leaders sit up at the front, we want to make sure they are comfortably familiar with the songs. We work with the individuals who will lead the different elements. Our adult Good-News Anchor spends time with each of the three reporters, going over the stories or interview questions. The puppeteers practice their scenes one last time. We go through the Theme for the Day and Sign for the Day with the children responsible for those elements. Then we go through the order of the service a couple of times to get a feel for the flow.

After rehearsal, we take all the materials, posters, storyboards, offering plates, puppets, bulletins, and so forth down to our worship space where we meet the ushers, greeters, and acolytes. We all spend the next ten minutes preparing the space and going over any last-minute details.

9:45 A.M., The Morning Of—*Children First* worship begins!

Worship Services

Provided in the following section is the Order of Worship for twelve different monthly services (plus one alternate), each with its own theme. You can select elements from the Song, Puppet-Script, and Prayer Appendices (see pages 56–95 and CD-ROM) to fashion the service you feel works best for your environment. In some cases a particular song, prayer, or script is recommended. Use what works best for you.

And feel free to move the different elements around. You may find that you get a better response by changing the order to fit your needs.

A slot for the Teaching Moment is included here to help you in your planning, even though we ourselves don't have one most of the time.

September
Learn

We chose the theme *Learn* to coincide with September back-to-school activities.

Prelude

Welcome and Announcements

Group Singing
"It's In the Book" (CD-ROM)
"The Bible Is Its Name-o" (CD-ROM)

Processional Hymn
"Thy Word Is a Lamp"

Prayer
Thank You, God, for Loving Us (page 85)

Theme for the Day: Learn

Sign of the Day: Learn

Good News
Possible interviews with three children asking them about something they learned over the summer or are looking forward to learning during the upcoming school year.

Expression of Faith
Puppet script: Gertrude (pages 60–61)

We Believe

Gloria Patri (page 19)

Musical Call to Prayer
"When We Take Time to Pray" (CD-ROM)

Time for Reflection

Focus on the idea that the more we learn about Jesus' life and teachings, the more we learn about God's love.

Lord's Prayer

Musical Prayer Response

"When We Take Time to Pray" (CD-ROM)

Scripture/Bible Story

Mark 4:1-2—Jesus the Teacher

Bible Memory Verse

Psalm 119:105—"Your word is a lamp to my feet and a light for my path."

Teaching Moment

Can be a children's sermon or the second scene from the puppet script: Gertrude (pages 60–61).

Offertory

Doxology

Prayer over the Gifts

All of My Treasures (page 86)

Closing Songs

"It's In the Book" (CD-ROM)
"Shalom" (CD-ROM)

Benediction

Postlude

October
Remember

Remember was our Communion-themed service, which took place the same month as World Communion Sunday.

Prelude

Welcome and Announcements

Group Singing
"A Special Meal" (CD-ROM)
"The Communion Union" (CD-ROM)
"We Remember You" (CD-ROM)

Processional Hymn
"Let Us Break Bread Together"

Prayer
Unlike Any Other (page 88)

Theme for the Day: Remember

Sign of the Day: Remember

Good News
Interviews with three children who are asked to think of a food that reminds them of a special time. (One child responded that every time he eats s'mores, he remembers a special camping trip he took with his dad.)

Expression of Faith
Puppet script: A Special Meal (pages 56–57)

We Believe

Gloria Patri

Musical Call to Prayer
The refrain to "We Remember You" (CD-ROM)

Time for Reflection
Focus on Communion as a special meal Jesus shared with his friends to help us remember God's love.

Lord's Prayer

Musical Prayer Response

The refrain to "We Remember You" (CD-ROM)

Scripture/Bible Story

Luke 22:19-20—The Lord's Supper

Bible Memory Verse

Luke 22:19b—"Do this in remembrance of me."

Teaching Moment

We celebrated Communion during this time. One of our ordained clergy led us in the following.

We remember that Jesus was the baby born at Christmas.
We remember Jesus.

We remember that Jesus loved the little children.
We remember Jesus.

We remember that Jesus is God's Son.
We remember Jesus.

We remember that Jesus taught us that God loves each one of us.
We remember Jesus.

We remember that Jesus shared a special meal with his friends.
We remember Jesus.

We remember that at the special meal, Jesus held up a loaf of bread. He thanked God for things to eat.

Then Jesus broke the bread into little pieces. He gave a piece of bread to each of his friends.
We remember Jesus.

We remember that at the special meal, Jesus held up a cup. He thanked God for things to drink. Then Jesus passed the cup to each of his friends.
We remember Jesus.

We remember Jesus whenever we drink juice and eat bread together at a special meal called Communion.
We remember Jesus.

We remember that Jesus said, "Do this in memory of me."
We remember Jesus.

(By Sharilyn S. Adair and Daphna Flegal © 1996 Cokesbury.)

The presiding minister used a Communion chalice and paten that had been created by a couple of children during a ceramics class at the church.

Offertory

Doxology

Prayer over the Gifts

All of My Treasures (page 86)

Closing Songs

"A Special Meal" (CD-ROM)

"Shalom" (CD-ROM)

Benediction

Postlude

November
Forever

The first Sunday in November was All Saints' Sunday. In this service, we did not shy away from the subjects of death and loss. But we made sure that the reassuring message through it all was that love does not die, but endures forever. In the past, we have done a November service on thankfulness the Sunday before Thanksgiving. This brings up a point. I recommend doing occasional *Children First* services on a different Sunday of the month. We have several children whose parents are no longer together, so they may be away from our church the first Sunday of the month.

Prelude

Welcome and Announcements

Group Singing
"Love Never Ends" (CD-ROM)
"1 Corinthians 13:8" (CD-ROM)

Processional Hymn
"Sing with All the Saints in Glory"

Prayer
For Loved Ones Who Have Died (page 92)

Theme for the Day: Forever

Sign of the Day: Forever

Good News
Interviews with three children, asking them to think of a wonderful time they wished could last forever.

Expression of Faith
Puppet script: Forever (pages 58–59)

We Believe

Gloria Patri

Musical Call to Prayer

"Love Never Ends," verse 1 (CD-ROM)

Time for Reflection

A continuation of the Good News. Invite all to think of a wonderful time in the past they wish would last forever. Reassure with the good news that, while those moments have come and gone, the memories, love, and goodwill remain. Love lasts forever.

Lord's Prayer

Musical Prayer Response

"Love Never Ends," verse 2 (CD-ROM)

Scripture/Bible Story

1 Corinthians 13:4-8a—The Way of Love

Bible Memory Verse

1 Corinthians 13:8a—"Love never ends."

Teaching Moment

Offertory

One of the children's choirs sang a piece about the enduring nature of God's love. Meanwhile, a slide show projected pictures of friends and family members of the children who had died or moved away.

Doxology

Prayer over the Gifts

All of My Treasures (page 86)

Closing Songs

"1 Corinthians 13:8" (CD-ROM)
"Shalom" (CD-ROM)

Benediction

Postlude

December
All

This service had a distinct "Christmas around the world" flavor.

Prelude

Welcome and Announcements

Group Singing
"Sing Noel" (CD-ROM)
"Mary Had a Baby" (CD-ROM)
"Away in a Manger" (CD-ROM)

Processional Hymn
"He Is Born"

Prayer
The text for "In the Bleak Midwinter," based on a poem by Christina Rossetti.

Theme for the Day: All

Sign of the Day: All

Good News
Three children report on gifts given across borders.

Expression of Faith
Puppet script: The Gift to Everyone (pages 62–63)

We Believe

Gloria Patri

Musical Call to Prayer
"A Star That Shines for Us All," verse 1 (CD-ROM)

Time for Reflection
Tell the story of the first performance of "Silent Night." (There are numerous books on this.) The carol, with its humble beginnings as a song sung by two men with a guitar in an Austrian village, is now cherished by people around the world. As a group, hum the tune to "Silent Night."

Lord's Prayer

Musical Prayer Response
"A Star That Shines for Us All," verse 2 (CD-ROM)

Scripture/Bible Story
Matthew 2:1b-2; 9b-11—The Visit from the Wise Men

Bible Memory Verse
Psalm 117:1—"Praise the LORD, all you nations!"

Teaching Moment

Offertory

Doxology

Prayer over the Gifts
All of My Treasures (page 86)

Closing Songs
"We Three Kings" (CD-ROM)
"Silent Night"

Benediction

Postlude

January
Different

Prelude

Welcome and Announcements

Group Singing
    "One of a Kind" (CD-ROM)
    "God Loves Everyone" (CD-ROM)

Processional Hymn
    "This Is My Song"

Prayer
    Thank You, God, for Different (page 90)

Theme for the Day: Different

Sign of the Day: Different

Good News
    Interviews with three children asking them to think of someone who is quite different from them, and why that's so cool.

Expression of Faith
    For this service, we had a group of recorder players illustrate the importance of playing their own, different parts. When they all played the melody, it sounded incomplete. When they all played the bass or tenor lines, it sounded boring. Only when each musician played his or her unique part did it create one whole, beautiful piece of music. This concept can also be demonstrated by singers using a hymn.

We Believe

Gloria Patri

Musical Call to Prayer
    refrain for "The Peacemakers" (CD-ROM)

Time for Reflection

Focus on how being different is okay. We often hear and say things like, "We're all just the same on the inside." Really? I have two daughters, born of the same parents and raised in the same environment. Let me tell you, they are different. And our whole family is blessed because of that.

The Time for Reflection *did, however, serve as a sort of pivot-point, as we started to gently turn to what we have in common. We are all children of a loving God, so we are all part of the same family.*

Lord's Prayer

Musical Prayer Response
refrain for "The Peacemakers" (CD-ROM)

Scripture/Bible Story
1 Corinthians 12:12-20, 26—Many Parts, One Body

Bible Memory Verse
1 Corinthians 12:20—"There are many members, yet one body."

Teaching Moment

Offertory

Doxology

Prayer over the Gifts
Thank You, God, for Same (page 90)

Closing Songs
"One of a Kind" (CD-ROM)
"Shalom" (CD-ROM)

Benediction

Postlude

February
Love

Prelude

Welcome and Announcements

Group Singing
"God Is Love" (CD-ROM)
"Jesus Loves Me" (CD-ROM)

Processional Hymn
"Love Divine, All Loves Excelling"

Prayer
I Am Loved (page 88)

Theme for the Day: Love

Sign of the Day: Love

Good News
Three children report, each on an act of love—one act of love in our world, one in our community, and one in our particular church family.

Expression of Faith
Puppet script: Tough Love (pages 64–65)

We Believe

Gloria Patri

Musical Call to Prayer
"Love Never Ends," verse 1 (CD-ROM)

Time for Reflection
A Tracing Prayer (page 94)

Lord's Prayer

Musical Prayer Response
"Love Never Ends," verse 2 (CD-ROM)

Litany of God's Love

When I'm feeling all alone,
God loves me.

When I'm staring far from home,
God loves me.

When I'm in the sun or rain,
God loves me.

When I'm feeling loss or pain,
God loves me.

This month we used the litany in lieu of a Bible story.

Bible Memory Verse

Deuteronomy 6:5—"You shall love the LORD your God with all your heart, and with all your soul, and with all your might."

Teaching Moment

We explored many different ways to show love besides saying, "I love you," such as helping family with chores, listening to a friend, saying "thank you" to God, and so forth.

Offertory

Doxology

Prayer over the Gifts

All of My Treasures (page 86)

Closing Songs

"God Is Love" (CD-ROM)
"Shalom" (CD-ROM)

Benediction

Postlude

March
Peer Pressure

Prelude

Welcome and Announcements

Group Singing
"I Have Decided to Follow Jesus" (CD-ROM)
"Exodus 23:2" (CD-ROM)

Processional Hymn
"Be Thou My Vision"

Prayer
We Will Follow Jesus (page 87)

Theme for the Day: Peer Pressure

Sign of the Day: Peer Pressure

Good News
Interview three children about a time when they felt pressured by others to do something they felt was wrong.

Expression of Faith
Puppet script: Peer Pressure (pages 66–67)

We Believe

Gloria Patri

Musical Call to Prayer
"When We Take Time to Pray," verse 1 (CD-ROM)

Time for Reflection
Explore what it means to do the "right" thing, even when others are doing the wrong thing. Also, can there be such a thing as positive peer pressure?

Lord's Prayer

Musical Prayer Response
"When We Take Time to Pray," verse 2 (CD-ROM)

Scripture/Bible Story
Luke 22:54-62—Peter Denies Jesus

Bible Memory Verse
Exodus 23:2, NIV— "Do not follow the crowd in doing wrong."

Teaching Moment

Offertory

Doxology

Prayer over the Gifts
All of My Treasures (page 86)

Closing Songs
"I Have Decided to Follow Jesus" (CD-ROM)
"Shalom" (CD-ROM)

Benediction

Postlude

April
Celebrate

Prelude

Welcome and Announcements

Group Singing
>"Hosanna to the King" (CD-ROM)
>"Blessed Is the One" (CD-ROM)

Processional Hymn
>"Hosanna, Loud Hosanna"

Prayer
>A Prayer for the Extraordinary (page 92)

Theme for the Day: Celebrate

Sign of the Day: Celebrate

Good News
>*Interview three children about a special celebration in each of their lives (birthday, Independence Day parade, and so forth).*

Expression of Faith
>*Child actors pantomimed different activities in preparation for a party, such as blowing up balloons, making a cake, hanging streamers, sending out invitations, and so forth. The worship participants got to guess what the actors were doing each time. The question at the end was, "What kind of party are they getting ready for?" No one guessed Palm Sunday.*

We Believe

Gloria Patri

Musical Call to Prayer
>"Be Still" (CD-ROM)

Time for Reflection
>*Explore some of the many celebrations we have each year. Recognize that Jesus entering our lives is truly worth celebrating.*

Lord's Prayer

Musical Prayer Response
    "Be Still" (CD-ROM)

Scripture/Bible Story
    Matthew 21:6-11—Jesus' Triumphal Entry

Bible Memory Verse
    Matthew 21:9—"Blessed is the one who comes in the name of the Lord!"

Teaching Moment

Offertory

Doxology

Prayer over the Gifts
    All of My Treasures (page 86)

Closing Songs
    "Hosanna to the King" (CD-ROM)
    "I Have Decided to Follow Jesus" (CD-ROM)

Benediction

Postlude

May
Prayer

Prelude

Welcome and Announcements

Group Singing
"The Lord's Prayer" (CD-ROM)
"When I Pray" (CD-ROM)

Processional Hymn
"It's Me, It's Me, O Lord (Standing in the Need of Prayer)"

Prayer
Thank You, God (page 87)
Because the theme was Prayer, *we had many different prayers scattered throughout the service.*

Theme for the Day: Prayer

Sign of the Day: Prayer

Prayer
A Wiggle Prayer (page 93)

Good News
Interview three children about a time they prayed, and why they did.

Expression of Faith
We had a painter who worked on a painted prayer throughout the service. During the Expression-of-Faith *segment, we asked her about her painting and why she felt that it was a painted prayer.*

We Believe

Gloria Patri

Prayer
When I Move and When I'm Still (page 85)

Musical Call to Prayer
"When We Take Time to Pray," verse 1 (CD-ROM)

Time for Reflection
We took a few deep breaths and then went right into the Bible story. The Scripture we chose was about Jesus teaching the disciples how to pray. We felt that it would make a perfect transition to go right from the Bible story into the Lord's Prayer.

Scripture/Bible Story
Luke 11:1-2a—The Disciples Ask Jesus to Teach Them How to Pray

Lord's Prayer
The Lord's Prayer is the continuation of the Scripture, Luke 11:2b-4.

Musical Prayer Response
"When We Take Time to Pray," verse 2 (CD-ROM)

Bible Memory Verse
1 Thessalonians 5:16-17—"Rejoice always, pray without ceasing."

Prayer
Help Me Be Softer (page 94)

Teaching Moment

Offertory

Doxology

Prayer over the Gifts
All of My Treasures (page 86)

Closing Songs
"The Lord's Prayer" (CD-ROM)
"Shalom" (CD-ROM)

Benediction

Postlude

June
Peace

Prelude

Welcome and Announcements

Group Singing
"The Peacemakers" (CD-ROM)
"Matthew 5:9" (CD-ROM)

Processional Hymn
"This Is My Song" *(This hymn is a congregational favorite, so it appears frequently.)*

Prayer
A Prayer for Peace (page 90)

Theme for the Day: Peace

Sign of the Day: Peace

Good News
Three children report on heroes in our world, our community, and our church, who actively work (or have worked) for peace.

Expression of Faith
Puppet script: Peace Out (pages 68–69)

We Believe

Gloria Patri

Musical Call to Prayer
refrain for "The Peacemakers" (CD-ROM)

Time for Reflection
Focus on peace on the inside and how it can greatly affect peace on the outside.

Lord's Prayer

Musical Prayer Response
       refrain for "The Peacemakers" (CD-ROM)

Scripture/Bible Story
       Isaiah 11:6-9—The Peaceable Kingdom

Bible Memory Verse
       Matthew 5:9—"Blessed are the peacemakers."

Teaching Moment

Offertory

Doxology

Prayer over the Gifts
       All of My Treasures (page 86)

Closing Songs
       "Matthew 5:9" (CD-ROM)
       "Shalom" (CD-ROM)

Benediction

Postlude

July
Share

Prelude

Welcome and Announcements

Group Singing
"Great Big God" (CD-ROM)
"Reach Out, Open Up, Share God's Love" (CD-ROM)

Processional Hymn
"For the Healing of the Nations"

Prayer
Enough to Share (page 84)

Theme for the Day: Share

Sign of the Day: Share

Good News
Interviews with three children about times they shared something (maybe even something they didn't, at first, want to share).

Expression of Faith
Puppet script: The Dog and the Bone (pages 70–71)

We Believe

Gloria Patri

Musical Call to Prayer
"Be Still" (CD-ROM)

Time for Reflection
Think about what it means to have enough. Are there those in the world who don't have enough? Do we have more than enough? What can we share?

Lord's Prayer

Musical Prayer Response
"Be Still" (CD-ROM)

Scripture/Bible Story

Based on John 6:1-15—Feeding the Five Thousand
We adapted this Bible story to make it interactive. The narrator reads aloud, and the worship participants make the appropriate body percussion and mouth sounds, as indicated.

One day Jesus crossed the Sea of Galilee. (*Make vocal wind sounds.*)

When he reached the other side, a huge crowd gathered to watch him cure the sick. (*Stomp in place to mimic the sound of walking feet.*)

As the sun began to set, the disciples said, "It is getting late and these people have nothing to eat." (*Descending whistle or "loo" sound.*)

"Then give them something to eat," Jesus replied. One of the disciples said to him, "There is a boy here who has five barley loaves and two fish. But what are they among so many people?" (*Clap five times. Make lip-pop sound twice.*)

Jesus said, "Make the people sit down." So the people, about five thousand in all, went to a grassy place and sat down. (*Rub hands together steadily to mimic sound of walking through grass.*)

Then Jesus took the loaves, and when he had given thanks, he broke the loaves and gave them to those who were seated. Then he did the same with the fish, as much as they wanted. (*Clap hands softly and continuously. Do the same with the lip-pops. Gradually get louder. Then all stop together.*)

When the people were full, Jesus told his disciples to gather all the leftover pieces. The disciples gathered enough pieces to fill twelve baskets. (*Make "mmm" sounds.*)

Bible Memory Verse

Psalm 23:1—"The LORD is my shepherd, I shall not want."

Teaching Moment

Offertory

Doxology

Prayer over the Gifts

All of My Treasures (page 86)

Closing Songs

"Reach Out, Open Up, Share God's Love" (CD-ROM)
"Shalom" (CD-ROM)

Benediction

Postlude

August
Anger Management

Prelude

Welcome and Announcements

Group Singing
  "Wiggle Praise" (CD-ROM)
  "You've Got to Learn to Let It Go" (CD-ROM)

Processional Hymn
  "Let There Be Peace on Earth"

Prayer
  Feelings Are Not Wrong (page 92)

Theme for the Day: Anger Management

Sign of the Day: Anger Management

Good News
  Interview three children about a time they were really angry, and what they did to cope with that anger. (If angry at a specific person, no naming names.)

Expression of Faith
  Spoon-Puppet Opera: Get a Handle on It! (pages 72–78, CD-ROM)

We Believe

Gloria Patri

Musical Call to Prayer
  refrain for "The Peacemakers" (CD-ROM)

Time for Reflection
  Explore some anger-management techniques, including stomping, counting, exercising, deep-breathing, praying, and others.

Lord's Prayer

Musical Prayer Response
    refrain for "The Peacemakers" (CD-ROM)

Scripture/Bible Story
    John 2:13-16—Jesus Cleanses the Temple

Bible Memory Verse
    Proverbs 16:32—"One who is slow to anger is better than the mighty."

Teaching Moment

Offertory

Doxology

Prayer over the Gifts
    All of My Treasures (page 86)

Closing Songs
    "You've Got to Learn to Let It Go" (CD-ROM)
    "Shalom" (CD-ROM)

Benediction

Postlude

Alternate
Neighbor

Prelude

Welcome and Announcements

Group Singing
"I've Got Helping Hands" (CD-ROM)
"Luke 10:27" (CD-ROM)

Processional Hymn
"For the Beauty of the Earth"

Prayer

Theme for the Day: Neighbor

Sign of the Day: Neighbor

Good News
Interview three children about a different neighbor. One child talks about a neighbor across the street. One child talks about a neighbor across town. One child talks about a neighbor across the sea.

Expression of Faith
Spoon-Puppet Opera: The New Girl (pages 79–82, CD-ROM)

We Believe

Gloria Patri

Musical Call to Prayer
refrain for "The Peacemakers" (CD-ROM)

Time for Reflection
Think of someone who may have treated us unfairly. Perhaps we are angry with this person, and that's okay. But can we recognize this person as a child of God and as our neighbor?

Lord's Prayer

Musical Prayer Response
refrain for "The Peacemakers" (CD-ROM)

Scripture/Bible Story
Luke 10:29-37—The Parable of the Good Samaritan

Bible Memory Verse
Matthew 22:39—"Love your neighbor as yourself."

Teaching Moment

Offertory

Doxology

Prayer over the Gifts
All of My Treasures (page 86)

Closing Songs
"I've Got Helping Hands" (CD-ROM)
"Shalom" (CD-ROM)

Benediction

Postlude

A Special Meal

Wendell and Razz

We wrote this script for our Children First *service on Holy Communion called* Remember. *We knew the puppeteer who plays Lorraine would be out of town, so we wrote for a new character, a surfer dude named Razz. The Razz story line continued into the following month's service when he has to move back to California.*

Scene: *Lunchroom. Razz is there already eating his lunch. Wendell enters. Both have lunch boxes.*

Wendell: Hi, can I sit here?

Razz: Of course, dude.

Wendell: I'm Wendell.

Razz: My name's Raspberry. But everyone just calls me "Razz."

Wendell: That sure looks like an interesting lunch.

Razz: Oh, dude! My mom is like totally radical! Check this out: a tofu burger on a whole wheat bun with a side of sprouts. It's healthy for me and healthy for the earth. Happy tummy, happy planet, dude.

Wendell: Sounds yummy. My mom packed me all my favorites. A PB and J with…crunchy peanut butter…woo-hoo! And lots of grape jelly! Also, a strawberry yogurt.

Razz: Sounds like your mom really takes care of you.

Wendell: Whenever I open my lunch box and see my favorite lunch, it reminds me how much my mom loves me. She always gives me just what I need.

Razz: Yeah, never thought of it that way; my mom always packs my favorites too. I think it's neat to have a special meal that reminds us how much we're loved. Hey, Wendell, I'll trade you half of my tofu burger for half of your PB and J.

Wendell: Great idea! I've never had a tofu burger before. Here. *(They exchange sandwich halves.)*

Razz: *(eating some of the PB and J)* This…*(munch…mumble…munch)*…is great.

Wendell: *(also eating)* And this is really good too! From now on, every time I eat a tofu burger I will think of my friend, Razz.

Razz: *(trying to get the words out, but mumbling terribly with all that sticky peanut butter)* And when I eat a PB and J, I'll think of you, Wendell.

Wendell: I'm not sure exactly what you just said, but it reminds me, we should probably go get some milk! *(The two walk off together.)*

Razz and Wendell

Forever

Wendell and Lorraine

This script was written for our Children First *service on the theme* Forever. *It took place on the first Sunday of November which happened to be All Saints' Sunday. We wanted to acknowledge that all of us have dealt with loss of some kind—a family member or pet dies, a dear friend moves away, a once-in-a-lifetime experience comes to an end. We wanted the message to be clear that loss will happen, but love lasts forever. We decided to use Razz as the friend who moves away. Since we had introduced Razz in the previous month's service, most of the worship participants would have at least some connection to the character, and hopefully be able to empathize with Wendell.*

(Wendell is onstage. Lorraine enters, bopping along...she passes Wendell once.)

Wendell: *(Sigh.)*

(Lorraine makes a second pass, still bopping.)

Wendell: *(Sigh.)*

(Lorraine makes one more pass.)

Wendell: *(Sigh.)*

Lorraine: Wendell, why so down in the dumps, dude?

Wendell: "Dude"...That's what Razz used to call me.

Lorraine: Razz, who's Razz?

Wendell: Razz is my new friend. I met him at lunch one day, and he shared his tofu burger with me.

Lorraine: He sounds cool. I'd love to meet him.

Wendell: I wish you could, but he's moved away.

Lorraine: Moved away?

Wendell: He moved back to California to go to surfing school.

Lorraine: Wow, California is far away, but that doesn't mean you can't still be friends.

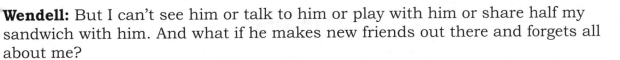

Wendell: But I can't see him or talk to him or play with him or share half my sandwich with him. And what if he makes new friends out there and forgets all about me?

Lorraine: Are you going to forget Razz?

Wendell: No, I'll never forget Razz.

Lorraine: Exactly. He's not going to forget you either.

Wendell: Even if I never see him again?

Lorraine: You don't need to see someone to remember the great times you shared together.

Wendell: Razz and I didn't know each other for very long, but we did have some fun times together.

Lorraine: It doesn't take long to make a memory that will really last.

Wendell: We've had some good times together, Lorraine. Do you think our friendship will last?

Lorraine: At least for another ten minutes!

Wendell: What? Huh?

Lorraine: Wendell...I'm kidding. Real friendship lasts forever.

Lorraine and Mr. Mark

Gertrude

Wendell and Human Friend

The script was written for our Children First *service on the theme* Learn, *on the first Sunday in September. Our puppeteer who plays Lorraine wasn't available, so we wrote this script for Wendell and a human actor, played by our talented children's choir director, Lindy. There is something very sweet about the interaction between a puppet and a live actor, provided the actor really focuses on the puppet, rather than the puppeteer. We also wrote this script in two short scenes, which would be separated by a few elements of the service to give the sense of the passage of time.*

Scene 1

(Wendell enters, very excited.)

Lindy: Hey, Wendell...you sure are excited; what's up?

Wendell: Oh, hey, Lindy. Tomorrow's the big day, a new school year!

Lindy: That does sound great!

Wendell: I can't wait to see my teacher again and be back in my classroom. I hope they haven't moved my desk. It was right next to Gertrude!

Lindy: Who's Gertrude?

Wendell: The class hamster, of course. I can watch her sleep in her cage and run on her exercise wheel.

Lindy: Wendell, you were in kindergarten last year, right?

Wendell: Yup!

Lindy: And tomorrow you start first grade, right?

Wendell: Yup!

Lindy: Well, that means you will have a new teacher.

Wendell: *(slightly bewildered)* A new teacher?

Lindy: And a new classroom.

Wendell: *(head hanging low)* Oh...but I like my old teacher and I want to be in my old classroom. I know where everything is in there.

Lindy: But Wendell...it's first grade. Think of all the amazing new things you will learn.

Wendell: But I don't want to learn new things...I want to sit next to Gertrude! *(Wendell walks off...mumbling...sad.)* Oh, Gertrude!

Scene 2

(Wendell enters; he's excited. Lindy is already in place.)

Lindy: Hey, Wendell, how was your first day in first grade?

Wendell: Amazing! I have a new teacher, and she's really nice. And I learned so much—like a square has two dimensions while a cube has three dimensions, and water freezes into ice at 32 degrees Fahrenheit, and how to say "Fahrenheit." *(practicing to himself)* Fahrenheit. Fahrenheit.

Lindy: Wow! Sounds like you learned some new things.

Wendell: Oh, and I can't wait to go back and learn a whole bunch more tomorrow. Wait...what happens if I go in one day and there isn't anything left to learn?

Lindy: Wendell, there will always be something new to learn.

Wendell: Even when I get as old as you?

Lindy: We spend our whole lives learning!

Wendell: Neat-o...I can't wait to tell Gertrude! Bye, Lindy.

Lindy: Bye, Wendell.

The Gift to Everyone

Wendell and Lorraine

This script was written for our Children First *service called* All, *which celebrated Christmas around the world. While we try to keep the puppet scripts from getting preachy, we couldn't resist the opportunity to weave in some Bible facts, with the help of Lorraine.*

(Lorraine is already onstage. She is excited, mumbling to herself, and about to explode with excitement. Wendell enters, also extremely excited.)

Lorraine: Wendell, I'm so glad you are here.

Wendell: I'm glad you are here too. I have something great to tell you!

Lorraine: Can't be any better than what I have to tell you!

Wendell: Let me tell first.

Lorraine: No, me first.

Wendell: No, me!

Both: I tried out for the Nativity play!

Both: I got cast as a wise man!

Both: Wait, you got cast as a wise man?

Both: So did I!

Both: That's so cool.

Both: *(realizing they are in sync)* Wait, how are we doing this?

Both: *(pause)* Antidisestablishmentarianism

Both: *(turning to look at the audience)* Whoa!

Lorraine: Well, I'm the wise man who brings the gold.

Wendell: Yeah, well I'm the one who brings the Frankenstein.

Lorraine: Frankenstein? I think you mean frankincense. It's a kind of resin used for making perfume and incense.

Wendell: Well, that doesn't sound like a very good gift for a baby. Oh, hey, I get to ride a camel! Are you going to ride a camel?

Lorraine: I'm riding an elephant.

Wendell: An elephant? Wise men didn't ride elephants!

Lorraine: Actually, in the Bible, it never said the wise men rode on camels.

Wendell: Really? So, the three wise men could have ridden different animals?

Lorraine: It never says in the Bible that there were three wise men either.

Wendell: Whoa! There could have been a whole bunch of them!

Lorraine: Could be; it says they came from the East guided by a star and brought gifts to the child.

Wendell: So it doesn't really matter what they rode on, how many there were, or the gifts they brought.

Lorraine: Exactly, because the wise men are there to remind people that Jesus came for everyone in the world—for all of us.

Wendell: Everyone in the world! Whoa, that's a lot of responsibility! I hope I don't get nervous carrying all that Frankenstein!

Lorraine: Oh, Wendell.

Tough Love

Wendell and Lorraine

This was our first Wendell-and-Lorraine script. As you'll notice, it's a little more talky-talk than our later scripts would become. We wrote this script for a Children First *service in February on the theme of* Love. *We wanted the children to begin to understand that love takes on many forms. And one of those forms is parental discipline. By the way, the parents at the service really appreciated this.*

(We see Lorraine already onstage; Wendell enters, head down, grumbling to himself.)

Wendell: Try to do something nice and what happens...

Lorraine: Wendell?

Wendell: *(still to himself)* I mean, how was I supposed to know she didn't want me to pull up those flowers?

Lorraine: Wendell?

Wendell: *(still to himself)* Parents, I just don't understand...

Lorraine: Wendell!!!!

Wendell: Oh, hi, Lorraine.

Lorraine: Wendell, what is the matter?

Wendell: Well, I wanted to do something for my mom's birthday. So I decided to have a parade, and I tried to make a parade float using my wagon and the flowers out of Mom's garden. And then I tied the wagon to my dog, Pasha. But when Mom came home, she got really mad because I picked all her flowers, and now she doesn't love me anymore.

Lorraine: Wait a second. She doesn't love you anymore? She said that?

Wendell: Well, no, but she was really mad at me and got really loud.

Lorraine: But that doesn't mean she doesn't love you.

Wendell: How do you know?

Lorraine: Remember when you let me play with your toy trains, and I broke them?

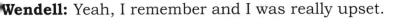

Wendell: Yeah, I remember and I was really upset.

Lorraine: But did you stop loving me?

Wendell: Of course not; I'll always love you. You're my best friend, Lorraine.

Lorraine: And…your mom will always love you. When you love someone, really love someone, you don't stop loving them.

Wendell: Yeah, but Mom was really upset!

Lorraine: Sometimes when people get upset with us it's because they love us so much, and they want us to do the right thing.

Wendell: Wow! Then my mommy must really, really love me because she was really, really upset!

Lorraine: Of course she loves you, and I love you too.

Wendell: I love you too. And you know, I'm going to go home and tell my mom I love her too! You want to come over later and play with my trains?

Lorraine: You mean the ones I broke?

Wendell: Mom got me a new one to make me feel better. Hey, she does love me! Bye, Lorraine.

Lorraine: Bye, Wendell.

Peer Pressure

Wendell and Lorraine

This script was written for a Children First *service on the theme of* Peer Pressure. *There's a lot more action, and we decided to spread it all out into three short scenes interspersed throughout the service.*

Scene 1
(Wendell is onstage, humming the music from the service.)

Lorraine: *(enters, walking backwards)* Hey, Wendell!

Wendell: *(looking at her)* Hey, Lorraine. What's going on?

Lorraine: *(walking backwards again, past Wendell)* Oh, nothing. What's going on with you?

Wendell: Um, why are you walking backwards?

Lorraine: Oh, "Backwards Walking"—"BW" we call it. It's the latest thing. Everyone's doing it.

Wendell: Why is everyone walking backwards?

Lorraine: 'Cause it's so cool.

Wendell: What makes it so cool?

Lorraine: 'Cause everyone is doing it. Hello?

Wendell: I'm not doing it.

Lorraine: You totally should; you'd fit right in.

Wendell: I...don't...know...

Lorraine: Well, think about it. *(exits, walking backwards)*

Scene 2
(Lorraine is waiting onstage.)

Wendell: *(enters, walking backwards)* Hey, Lorraine, I've been practicing. I'm doing the "BW"!

Lorraine: Oh, Wend-oodle, that is so last week-oodle!

Wendell: *(turning now to face her)* What?

Lorraine: You heard me-oodle.

Wendell: Why are you saying "oodle" after everything?

Lorraine: Wend-oodle, it's the latest-oodle to doodle!

Wendell: Well, it sounds silly.

Lorraine: Everyone is doodling it.

Wendell: Why?

Lorraine: 'Cause it's way coodle, for shoodle!

Wendell: Well, I don't know…

Lorraine: Think about it. See you tomm-oodle. Goodb-oodle! *(Lorraine exits.)*

Scene 3

Wendell: *(onstage, trying to practice "oodling")* My name is…Wend-oodle…and I'm so cool-oodle…*(sigh)* This is what it takes to fit in?

Lorraine: *(enters, bouncing this time)*

Wendell: Hey, Lorraine…um…oodle…

Lorraine: *(she continues to bounce in place as she talks to Wendell)* Oh, Wendell, that is so yesterday. The latest thing is "Bouncing." You should do it!

Wendell: Wait, "Bouncing" is now the new thing?

Lorraine: Uh-huh!

Wendell: Do you even like doing it?

Lorraine: Doesn't matter. Gotta fit in!

Wendell: Why do something just to fit in, if you don't like what you are doing?

Lorraine: *(struggling to explain)* Well, you see…um…it's…I… *(stops bouncing)* I don't know. *(catching her breath)* I was doing it so people would like me.

Wendell: You don't have to do all that stuff. I like you for who you are.

Lorraine: Oh, you have to say that because you are my best friend.

Wendell: Well, what friend would I be if I made you do things you didn't like to do?

Lorraine: Not a very good one! *(She has an "aha" moment.)* Oh…I see.

Wendell: There is only one thing you need to do to fit in with me…be yourself.

Lorraine: I can definitely do that!

Peace Out

Wendell and Lorraine

This script was written for our Children First service on the theme of Peace. Wendell and Lorraine demonstrate how a situation can really escalate, until two parties are angry with one another and they can't even remember why.

(Wendell is playing air guitar while humming a rock song...when in bops Lorraine.)

Lorraine: Hey, Wendell. What are you doing?

Wendell: Playing air guitar...wait, wait, here comes the big solo. *(plays)*

Lorraine: You call that air guitar? Step aside. Let me show you how it's done. *(She plays air guitar while humming a country/western song.)*

Wendell: Not bad...for a beginner! Time to crank it up to 10! *(plays)*

Lorraine: 10, huh? Well, I go to 11! *(plays)*

Wendell: Yeah, but does your air guitar have a whammy bar? *(plays with pretend whammy bar)*

Lorraine: Wendell...?

(Wendell continues playing.)

Lorraine: Wendell...?

(Wendell is really getting into it.)

Lorraine: Weeennnnnddddddeeeellllll!!!!!!!!

Wendell: *(stops playing)* Huh?

Lorraine: What are we doing here?

Wendell: Playing air guitar, dude!

Lorraine: I wouldn't call what we're doing "playing." It feels more like fighting.

Wendell: Yeah...it does feel kind of like fighting. How did that happen?

Lorraine: Well…you were playing air guitar, and I came along and tried to do better than you, and you tried to be better than me, and back and forth until it wasn't fun anymore.

Wendell: What's the point of playing air guitar if you're not having fun? Hey, Lorraine, you want to play "together"?

Lorraine: Sure. What was the first riff you were jammin' on?

Wendell: What, this one? *(plays)*

Lorraine: Yeah, yeah, keep going. *(She joins in.)*

(Big finish…they stop.)

Lorraine: You rock, Wendell!

Wendell: No, Lorraine…we rock! Peace out!

Lorraine: Peace out, Wendell.

Lorraine and Mr. Mark

The Dog and the Bone

This Threadbare-Theatre script was adapted from a school show we did based on Aesop's Fables. *This scene can be performed by one narrator and one puppeteer or one very talented puppeteer.* The Dog and the Bone *was performed for a service on sharing, and illustrates the difference between enough and too much.*

Narrator: Now we come to the fab fable of *The Dog and the Bone*. For this fable, we're going to need the help of Lucy. Lucy, you are going to play the dog. Here is your bone. Now hold onto it, and don't let it go, okay?

Lucy: *(mumbling)* Okay.

Narrator: We're also going to need the help of you in the audience. This fable has a call-and-response feel to it. I'll say part of the story, and then you respond with: "Oh, yeah. Uh-huh. Oh, yeah. Oh, yeah. Uh-huh." Got it? Well, we'll find out. Here we go with *The Dog and the Bone*.

Lucy was a dog with a big juicy bone.
(Response.)
She trotted down a path happy and alone.
(Response.)
She walked across a bridge, looking over the side.
(Response.)
A dog with another bone is what she spied.
(Response.)
Her happy, peaceful thoughts turned to something new.
(Response.)
Why should she have one bone when she could have two?
(Response.)
She thought and she thought how to get the other bone.
(Response.)
She really wanted both bones to be her own.
(Response.)

Then, Lucy got an idea. She would make the other dog drop its bone. Then she would take it for herself.

First, Lucy challenged the other dog to a staring contest. She stared and stared, without blinking once. But the other dog didn't blink either.

Lucy made a mean face. So did the other dog.

She made a silly face. So did the other dog.

"This isn't working at all," thought Lucy.

So she stood on her tiptoes to make herself look big and intimidating. The other dog stood on its tiptoes and looked just as big, and just as intimidating.

Lucy tried snarling and growling. But everything she tried, the other dog did.

Finally, Lucy decided to bark ferociously and scare the other dog into letting go of its bone. So she did. And do you know what happened?

Lucy's bone fell, splash!, right into the water. That wasn't another dog with another bone. It was Lucy's own reflection in the pond.

No longer was she happy, she had turned to greed.
(Response.)
By going after something that she didn't need.
(Response.)
She didn't have two bones. She didn't have one.
(Response.)
She tried to have it all, but she ended up with none.
(Response.)
The moral of the story, the purpose of the plot—
(Response.)
There's no need for greed. Just be glad with what you've got.
(Response.)
(Response.)
(Response.)

Lucy and Wendell

Get a Handle on It!

An Opera for Spoon Puppets

As the narration is read, have the puppeteers use the puppets to pantomime the actions. The primary actions are printed in bold in the narration. The narration may be spoken by one narrator or by several.

Narrator 1: Today we visit the Verdi family. It is almost time for dinner. Mr. and Mrs. Verdi are in the kitchen, busily preparing a Mexican feast.

Mrs. Verdi is **flipping tortillas** on the griddle, while Mr. Verdi is **chopping onions** for the pico de gallo.

Narrator 2: The wonderful smells float into the dining room where two of the Verdi children, Figaro and Violetta, are **setting the table**.

Suddenly, there is a WHAM as the front door swings open and the third Verdi child, Billy Joe, **storms in**.

Narrator 3: Mrs. Verdi **comes into** the dining room to see what all the fuss is about. Billy Joe tells her that he is **hopping mad** that he did not get picked to start for his school's basketball team, the Mighty Bananas.

Violetta **hands him a vase** and tells him to throw it—it will make him feel better.

Mrs. Verdi has a different idea, and she **takes the vase** from Billy Joe.

Song 1: "Take a Breath"
(page 74, CD-ROM)

Narrator 4: So Billy Joe **takes a deep breath** and **counts to ten**. Though he's a little more relaxed, he's still pretty angry.

Just then, Mr. Verdi **bursts through the kitchen door in tears**. Apparently the onions have finally gotten to him. The rest of the Verdis tell him about Billy Joe.

Narrator 5: Mr. Verdi assures Billy Joe that it's okay to be angry. He then suggests some ways to let off some steam.

Song 2: "Let Off Some Steam"
(pages 75–76, CD-ROM)

Narrator 6: Billy Joe tries some of his dad's suggestions. He **jogs in place, plays some air guitar,** and **spins around**.

Narrator 7: He admits that he does feel better. His parents taught him some good ways to release his anger, but they also listened to him. They didn't make him feel like his anger was wrong.

Puppet Scripts

Song 3: "I Feel Better"
(pages 77–78, CD-ROM)

Narrator 8: The Verdis **sat down** and **enjoyed a hearty Mexican feast**. Mr. and Mrs. Verdi were proud of the lesson Billy Joe learned that day—

There's nothing wrong with getting stirred
up from time to time.
It's how you "handle" it that counts.

Violetta, Figaro, Mrs. Verdi, Mr. Verdi

Take a Breath

WORDS: Mark Burrow
MUSIC: Mark Burrows, based on Haydn's Surprise Symphony mvmt. II

Let Off Some Steam

Third time to Coda

WORDS: Mark Burrow
MUSIC: Mark Burrows, based on Rossini's *William Tell Overture*

I Feel Better

WORDS: Mark Burrow
MUSIC: Mark Burrows, based on Handel's *Hallelujah Chorus*

man - y ways __ to get a grip. He feels bet - ter, so much bet - ter. He feels

bet - ter, so much bet - ter. He feels bet - ter.
(I feel)

Puppet Scripts

The New Girl

An Opera for Spoon Puppets

As the narration is read, have the puppeteers use the puppets to pantomime the actions. The primary actions are printed in bold in the narration. The narration may be spoken by one narrator or by several.

Narrator 1: Today we visit the Verdi family. It is almost time for dinner, and Mr. and Mrs. Verdi are in the kitchen busily preparing an Indian feast. Mrs. Verdi is **stirring the basmati rice** while Mr. Verdi is **chopping spinach**.

Narrator 2: The wonderful smells float into the dining room where the Verdi children, Figaro, Violetta, and Billy Joe, are **setting the table**. Violetta is **shaking her head** and venting about the new girl at school.

Song 1: "That Girl Is Really Gross"
(page 80, CD-ROM)

Narrator 3: Just then, Mr. and Mrs. Verdi **enter the dining room** loaded down with bowls and platters of mouthwatering eats. They have overheard Violetta's concerns about the new girl. Figaro suggests **pelting the new girl** with cold Brussels sprouts. Mr. Verdi has a different idea.

Song 2: "The New Girl in Your School"
(page 81, CD-ROM)

Narrator 4: Violetta still isn't sure. What if the new girl still won't be her friend? But she agrees to try.

Narrator 5: The Verdi family **sits down** and enjoys a wonderful meal. Mr. and Mrs. Verdi are proud of their daughter for agreeing to do the right thing, even though it's difficult.

Song 3: "Love Our Neighbors"
(page 82, CD-ROM)

Narrator 6: So Violetta **goes to school** the next day with a renewed desire to make friends with the new girl. What do you think happens?

The End.

That Girl Is Really Gross

WORDS: Mark Burrow
MUSIC: "La donna é mobile" from Verdi's *Rigoletto;* arranged by Mark Burrow

Words and arr. © 2005 Abingdon Press, admin. by The Copyright Co., Nashville, TN 37212

The New Girl in Your School

1. When you see her in the hall do not make her feel small.
2. Take the time to un-der-stand. Of-fer a friend-ly hand.

It won't help at all to reach the new girl in your school.
Let your mind ex-pand to reach the new girl in your school.

Think of her each time you pray. Think of kind things to say.

Find a lov-ing way to reach the new girl in your school.

WORDS: Mark Burrow
MUSIC: "In the Hall of the Mountain King" from *Peer Gynt Suite I* by Grieg; arranged by Mark Burrows
Words and arr. © 2005 Abingdon Press, admin. by The Copyright Co., Nashville, TN 37212

Love Our Neighbors

WORDS: Mark Burrow
MUSIC: *Oh, Susanna!* by Stephen Foster; arranged by Mark Burrow

The Verdi family relaxes after a performance.

Prayers

This small prayer collection includes many different prayer styles, such as poem prayers, unison prayers, responsive prayers, action prayers, and breath prayers. The prayers cover many themes, including love, individuality, peace, grudges, loss, sharing, and much more. Many prayers are appropriate for more than one occasion. Feel free to use whichever prayers you think fit best for your setting. And invite children to create their own prayers to contribute to worship.

Unison Poem Prayers

We Can Follow God's Own Way

God is caring.
God is kind—
Giving love
And peace of mind.

We can follow
God's own way
By sharing, caring
Every day. Amen.

Enough to Share

Sometimes the things we have to do
Aren't easy, quick, or fun.
But God will be there at the start,
And when our task is done.

God fills our lives with hope and love,
But doesn't stop right there;
God always gives us extra so
We'll have enough to share. Amen.

You Have Sent Your Spirit

I will never doubt the things
I know but cannot see;
For you have sent your Spirit,
And it's found a home in me.

I will praise your name in song,
Though I may sing off-key;
For you have sent your Spirit,
And it's found a home in me.

Even in my times of stress,
My heart is ever free;
For you have sent your Spirit,
And it's found a home in me. Amen.

By Name

Some of us are short.
Some of us are tall.
Some of us perform ballet.
Some of us play ball.

Everyone is different,
But one thing stays the same—
God loves every one of us
And knows us all by name. Amen.

When I Move and When I'm Still

Sometimes life can move so fast.
Every hour goes rushing past.
Music lessons, homework, chores—
Can my body take much more?

Then I find a quiet place,
Take a breath and pray for grace.
God helps me and always will,
When I move
And when I'm still. Amen.

I May Be Young

I may be young.
I may be small.
But I can listen
To God's call.

I will follow.
God will lead
As I help
All those in need. Amen.

When I Show My Love

I can love and honor God
In many different ways;
I can pray a silent prayer,
Or shout my thanks and praise.

I can dance and leap and play,
Or sing a simple song.
God likes it when I show my love,
For love is never wrong. Amen.

Thank You, God, for Loving Us

Thank you, God, for starlit nights,
And sunny, joy-filled days.
Thank you, God, for loving us,
And teaching us your ways.

Thank you, God, for soaring birds
Who daily sing your praise.
Thank you, God, for loving us,
And teaching us your ways.

Thank you, God, for listening
To every prayer we raise.
Thank you, God, for loving us,
And teaching us your ways. Amen.

When We Take Time to Pray

Sometimes we lose direction,
And we can't find our way.
But God will guide us through it
When we take time to pray.

Sometimes we feel that no one
Hears what we have to say.
But God will always listen
When we take time to pray.

We know that God is with us,
Helping us through each day.
God will take time to be there
When we take time to pray. Amen.

All of My Treasures

All of my treasures
I joyfully give—
The prayers that I whisper,
The life that I live.
My time and my talents,
My hands and my heart—
God gave all these to me,
Now I'll do my part. Amen.

Just the Way We Are

If God didn't want us to laugh,
We wouldn't have been made so
giggly.

If God didn't want us to move,
We wouldn't have been made so
wiggly.

If God didn't want us to give,
We wouldn't have been made so
sharing.

If God didn't want us to love,
We wouldn't have been made so
caring.

Thank you, God, for making us just
the way we are. Amen.

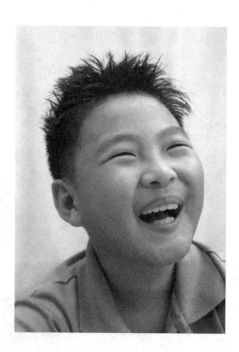

We Will Follow Jesus

Will you follow Jesus?
We will follow Jesus.

Even when times are tough?
We will follow Jesus.

Even when things get rough?
We will follow Jesus.

Even when days are dreary?
We will follow Jesus.

Even when you feel weary?
We will follow Jesus. Amen.

Thank You, God

For love you share—
Thank you, God.

For hearts to care—
Thank you, God.

For peace you bring—
Thank you, God.

For everything—
Thank you, God. Amen.

How Can I Keep from Loving?

When I spend time with my family—
How can I keep from smiling?

When I hear my favorite song—
How can I keep from singing?

When I play with my best friend—
How can I keep from laughing?

When I think about my many blessings—
How can I keep from dancing?

When I think of how much I am loved—
How can I keep from loving? Amen.

Up

Whenever I feel small,
Your love lifts me **up**.

Whenever I feel low,
Your love cheers me **up**.

Whenever I feel outnumbered,
Your love backs me **up**.

Whenever I feel worn out,
Your love wakes me **up**.

Whenever I feel empty,
Your love fills me **up**. Amen.

With

Whenever I feel afraid,
I know courage is with me.

Whenever I feel alone,
I know love is with me.

Whenever I feel frustrated,
I know patience is with me.

Whenever I feel unhappy,
I know joy is with me.

I can handle whatever life brings,
Because I know God is with me.
God is always with me. Amen.

I Am Loved

Before your first breath—
I am loved.

After your last heartbeat—
I am loved.

Through every breath and heartbeat
in between—
I am loved. *(breath)*

I am loved. *(breath)*
I am loved. *(breath)* **Amen.**

Unlike Any Other

This is a day unlike any other.
A day to remember God's love.

This is a place unlike any other.
A day to remember God's love.

Communion is a meal unlike any
other.
**A day to remember God's love.
Amen.**

Love Lives

Leader: Trees may fall,
Children: But faith stands.

Leader: Flowers may fade,
Children: But hope lasts.

Leader: Loved ones may die,
Children: But love lives.

All: Their love lives forever.
Our love lives forever.
God's love lives forever. Amen.

Alive!

Christ is alive!
Hallelujah!

Love is alive!
Hallelujah!

Hope is alive!
Hallelujah!

We are alive!
Hallelujah! Amen!

God Is Always with Me

Leader: In the morning, warm and bright,
Children: In the middle of the night,
All: God is always with me. God is always there.
Leader: When my heart is full of song,
Children: When I put my shoes on wrong,
All: God is always with me. God is always there.
Leader: When I'm leading in the race,
Children: When I'm running in last place,
All: God is always with me. God is always there.
Leader: In my classroom, church, or home,
Children: With my friends, or on my own,
All: God is always with me. God is always there. Amen.

Ready, Willing, and Able

Are you ready to hear what God has in store for us today?
We are ready.

Are you willing to follow where Jesus leads?
We are willing.

Are you able to feel the Spirit that joins us as one family of love?
We are able.

Thank you, God, for this new day, full of opportunities to serve you and your people.
We are ready, willing, and able. Amen.

Thank You, God, for Different

Some are short; some are tall.
Thank you, God, for different.

Some play banjo; some play ball.
Thank you, God, for different.

Some are quiet; some make noise.
Thank you, God, for different.

Some are girls, and some are boys.
Thank you, God, for different.

Some like pizza; some like yam.
Thank you, God, for different.

Some like honey; some like jam.
**Thank you, God, for different.
Amen.**

Thank You, God, for Same

We all share the stars above.
Thank you, God, for same.

We all share your endless love.
Thank you, God, for same.

We all feel the sun and rain.
Thank you, God, for same.

We all feel life's joy and pain.
Thank you, God, for same.

We are family through your Son.
Thank you, God, for same.

We are many; we are one.
Thank you, God, for same. Amen.

A Prayer for Peace

Person 1: Amani.
Person 2: Paz.
Together: A prayer for peace.

Person 1: Heiwa.
Person 2: Mir.
Together: A prayer for peace.

Person 1: Pace.
Person 2: Shanti.
Together: A prayer for peace.

Person 1: Eyewi.
Person 2: Shalom.
Together: A prayer for peace. Amen.

Amani	ah-MAH-nee	*(Swahili)*
Paz	PAHS	*(Spanish)*
Heiwa	HEY-wah	*(Japanese)*
Mir	MEER	*(Russian)*
Pace	PAH-cheh	*(Italian)*
Shanti	SHAHN-tee	*(Hindi)*
Eyewi	eh-YEH-wee	*(Nez Perce—Native American)*
Shalom	shah-LOHM	*(Hebrew)*

The individual words for peace may be spoken by eight different people or by everyone in unison. Also, if the children know how to say peace in other languages, invite them to share these in the prayer.

Unison Prayers

Hugging God

Dear God,
I love you so much that sometimes
I want to reach out and hug you.

But how can I get my arms around you
when you're so big?

Bigger than a whale's splash.
Bigger than a mountain.
Big enough to reach the farthest stars in
the sky.

For now, I'll simply hold my arms out
wide, happy to know that you are
hugging me. Amen.

Holding God

Dear God,
I love you so much that sometimes
I want to hold you.

But how can I hold you
When you're so small?

Smaller than an eyelash.
Smaller than a caterpillar's footprint.
Small enough to reach the deepest, just-
for-me places in my heart.

For now, I'll simply wrap my arms snugly
around myself, happy to know that you
are holding me. Amen.

God Hears Them All

Songs loud and proud!
And also the soft.
Words long and strong!
And also the whisper.

Prayers low and slow.
And also the silent.

Every song,
Every word,
Every prayer—

God's ears hear them all.
God's heart cherishes them all.
Amen.

A Prayer for the Extraordinary

Gracious God, you sent Jesus to teach us of your love.

He was born in a stable and raised as a humble carpenter's son. Those around him, who didn't know him better, might even have thought he was ordinary.

Please help us be open to your love and the promise that, in your hands, the ordinary can be extraordinary. Amen.

I Know How to Say, "I Love You"

Dear God, I may have a hard time saying things like Mephibosheth, Nebuchadnezzar, and Thessalonica. But I know how to say, "I love you." I know how to say, "I'm sorry." I know how to say, "Thank you." And I know how to say, "Amen."

The Face of God

Loving God,
Help us to see you in the faces
Of people we meet each day;
And help the people we meet each day
To see your face in us. Amen.

For Loved Ones Who Have Died

Dear God, today we pray for loved ones who have died:
For those who taught us,
For those who made us laugh,
For those who made us feel safe,
For those who made us feel loved,
For those who made us feel at home.

Thank you for all the joy their lives have brought us, and in our sadness, help us to know that:
They are forever safe,
They are forever loved,
And they are forever at home with you.
Amen.

Feelings Are Not Wrong

Sometimes I feel happy,
And feelings are not wrong.
Sometimes I feel sad,
And feelings are not wrong.
Sometimes I feel angry,
And feelings are not wrong.

Thank you, God, for giving us
So many powerful feelings.
Thank you also for giving us the power
To show our feelings in healthy ways,
So that we don't hurt others,
Or ourselves. Amen.

Prayers

Action Prayers

A Wiggle Prayer

O God, who made my fingers,
(wiggle fingers)

O God, who made my toes,
(wiggle toes)

O God, who made my eyebrows,
(wiggle eyebrows)

O God, who made my nose,
(wiggle nose)

You made my heart for laughter,
(put hand to heart)

You made my voice for song,
(make "singing" pose)

You made my soul to dance,
(dance in place)

And praise you all life long.
(raise both hands in the air)

Amen.

A Simple Prayer for Peace

Take in a deep breath through the nose.
Then sigh out softly through the mouth.
With your last bit of breath, whisper the
word "peace."

*Note: This can be done with other single
words, such as* grace, patience,
kindness, love, friendship, or
forgiveness.

A Grudge Prayer

Think of someone who has recently
made you angry, upset, or has hurt your
feelings.

Place an open hand over your heart and
rub until you feel the "grudge" come to
the surface.

Close your hand around the grudge,
then lift your hand away from your
heart. Open your hand and blow the
grudge into the air.

*(Conclude by saying the
following phrase:)*

God forgives, and so can I.
I forgive. Amen.

A Tracing Prayer

Think of someone you love.
Trace the first initial (or the entire name) of that person onto the palm of your hand.
Then, hold that hand to your heart and say the word "love."

Note: This kind of prayer can also be helpful when praying for someone you hope to love or are having a hard time learning to love.

Help Me Be Softer

HELP ME BE SOFTER, LORD!
(Make your voice softer as you say each phrase.)
Help me be softer, Lord.
Help me be softer, Lord.
Help me be softer, Lord,
so I can hear you better. Amen.

Help Me Slow Down

Help me slow down, Lord.
Help *(breath)* me slow down, Lord.
Help *(breath)* me *(breath)* slow down, Lord.
Help *(breath)* me *(breath)* slow *(breath)* down, Lord.
Help *(breath)* me *(breath)* slow *(breath)* down *(breath)*, Lord.
Help *(breath)* me *(breath)* slow *(breath)* down *(breath)*, Lord *(breath)*.
Amen. *(breath...breath...breath)*

Praying Hands

I put my hands together every evening
when I pray.
(Put hands together.)

But think of all the special ways I use
my hands each day.
*(Point to side of head to indicate
"thinking.")*

Each morning I reach down to tie my
little brother's shoes.
*(Reach down and pretend to tie another
person's shoes.)*

I clap for our school's ball team. I
support them, win or lose.
(Clap.)

I feed my puppy every day, and scratch
behind his ears.
(Pretend to scratch a puppy's ears.)

I even raise my hand in class when they
need volunteers.
(Raise hand.)

Whenever my best friend feels sad, I pat
her on the back.
(Pat.)

She comes to my house after school. I
make us both a snack.
(Pretend to make a PB and J.)

On weekends I help Mom and Dad with
little household chores.
I help Mom fold the laundry,
(Pretend to fold a shirt.)

And I help Dad mop the floors.
(Pretend to mop.)

I stir soup in the kitchen where the
needy come to eat.
(Pretend to stir a pot.)

I shake the hands and learn the names
of all the friends I meet.
(Pretend to shake hands.)

God listens as I pray each night. God's
hands can ease my cares.
(Put hand to ear.)

Then God works though my hands to
answer someone else's prayers.
*(Point to self, then put hands back
together.)*

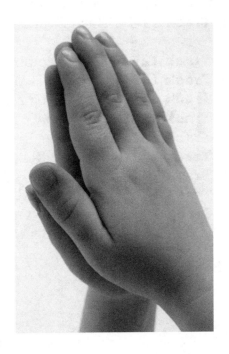

Music on CD-ROM

Track 1	A Special Meal
Track 2	A Star That Shines for Us All
Track 3	Away in a Manger
Track 4	Be Still
Track 5	Blessed Is the One
Track 6	God Is Love
Track 7	God Loves Everyone
Track 8	Great Big God
Track 9	Hosanna to the King
Track 10	I Feel Better
Track 11	I Have Decided to Follow Jesus
Track 12	I've Got Helping Hands
Track 13	It's In the Book
Track 14	Jesus Loves Me
Track 15	Let Off Some Steam
Track 16	Love Never Ends
Track 17	Love Our Neighbors
Track 18	Mary Had a Baby
Track 19	One of a Kind
Track 20	Reach Out, Open Up, Share God's Love
Track 21	Shalom
Track 22	Sing Noel
Track 23	Take a Breath
Track 24	That Girl Is Really Gross
Track 25	The Bible Is Its Name-o
Track 26	The Lord's Prayer
Track 27	The New Girl in Your School
Track 28	The Peacemakers
Track 29	We Remember You
Track 30	We Three Kings
Track 31	When We Take Time to Pray
Track 32	Wiggle Praise
Track 33	You've Got to Learn to Let It Go

Sheet Music Only

1 Corinthians 13:8
Exodus 23:2
Luke 10:27
Matthew 5:9
The Communion Union
When I Pray

CD-ROM